Miss

People

True Stories of Unexplained Disappearances

(True Stories of People Gone Missing and Never Found)

Randall Cornett

Published By **Adan Kalcanto**

Randall Cornett

All Rights Reserved

Missing People: True Stories of Unexplained Disappearances (True Stories of People Gone Missing and Never Found)

ISBN   978-1-77485-730-4

Legal & Disclaimer

The information contained in this ebook is not designed to replace or take the place of any form of medicine or professional medical advice. The information in this ebook has been provided for educational & entertainment purposes only.

The information contained in this book has been compiled from sources deemed reliable, and it is accurate to the best of the Author's knowledge; however, the Author cannot guarantee its accuracy and validity and cannot be held liable for any errors or omissions. Changes are periodically made to this book. You must consult your doctor or get professional medical advice before using any of the suggested remedies, techniques, or information in this book.

Upon using the information contained in this book, you agree to hold harmless the Author from and against any damages, costs, and expenses, including any legal fees potentially resulting from the application of any of the information provided by this guide. This disclaimer applies to any damages or injury caused by the use and application, whether directly or indirectly, of any advice or information presented, whether for breach of contract, tort, negligence, personal injury, criminal intent, or under any other cause of action.

You agree to accept all risks of using the information presented inside this book. You need to consult a professional medical practitioner in order to ensure you are both able and healthy enough to participate in this program.

TABLE OF CONTENTS

INTRODUCTION

In 2012 The Wall Street Journal reported that around 8 million people are reported missing each year. Some are discovered within hours, while others are found within days, others in a matter of weeks. Lastly, some individuals are discovered after months of being missing. But, the tale is not always a happy one. Of the millions that disappear each year across the globe There are also those who vanish completely and never return. The huge number of people that disappear every year is when looked at in depth scary. This book we'll look at several of the more frightening and touching, bizarre and frightening stories.

Families, friends as well as loved ones, are on the list of people who have been added to the ever-growing list of missing persons. For those separated from their loved ones, the news get more desperate and chaotic. The emotional turmoil that incident can create is extremely difficult to manage, with no being able to decide whether to grieve or keep hope. Amid a vast void of fear the people who are close to the person who is missing are usually the most crucial to the search , and often the most suspect.

In general, they are those who have the vast amount of information that authorities require in order to make any progress in the investigation into the location of the suspect.
However, the reasons disappearances can differ significantly. As we'll see throughout the book it is not the case that there is any standard or usual type of disappearance. For those who are reported missing, determining whether they've fled or been abducted, fallen victim to an accident or even killed, is often a challenge. There is a lack of evidence to come from and numerous sources to offer an explanation, the investigation can get complicated and scattered over many years. Due to this, a number of missing person cases remain unsolved and waiting for that last clue that could end the case and let those who are missing feel a the satisfaction of having closure.

One of the most troubling situations are those where there's no obvious reason of the reason for disappearance. In certain instances the search for an explanation that is almost impossible. When people are eager to appeal to the supernatural or the bizarre or the bizarre, as well as the supernatural to explain the disappearance of their loved ones the theories proposed are usually too absurd to be real. It's only that when we analyze the evidence and realize that rational explanations are exhausted that we begin to look at the possibility of mysterious and abstract explanations for the disappearance of people, women and even children. Only after exhausting the logic possibility of the possibility that something is beyond the norm.

Through this book, we'll try to look at the wide range of cases that have fascinated those who were interested and enraged by the people affected for years. Some of these cases were public stories, and others are still private tragedy. When it comes to missing people, trying to discover the cause is nearly impossible as finding the missing person. Join us on this adventure and discover how captivating and fascinating the stories of missing persons can be.

CHAPTER 1: A CRIMINAL MASTERMIND THAT VANISHED AFTER JUMPING OFF THE PLANE

Who: D.B. Cooper

Date when: November 24 November, 1971

What is the airspace between Portland and Seattle

Context

The most well-known case of missing persons of American time, the tale of D. B. (or Dan) Cooper involves the heist of a criminal and a thrilling escape and a enduring mythology. If you've ever thought of making a huge amount or the perfect crime and that disappearance story of Cooper is the one that you can aspire to.

That day

It's as follows. The day before Christmas in 1971, a person calling Dan Cooper was spotted on the street. Dan Cooper got onto Flight 305 on Northwest Airlines, which was intended travel across the state of Portland up to Seattle. The information available at the time showed him in a dark suit, with a tie of black witnesses stating that he was an executive or businessman of some sort. While on the plane, Cooper gestured towards his briefcase, showing the flight attendant the bomb that was smuggled onto. With this bomb, Cooper seized the plane. The plane was then forced to arrive in Seattle in which the hijacker demanded $200,000 money, 4 parachutes as well as enough food to feed his crew and himself. The passengers were freed and the plane took into the sky with Cooper along with the cash as well as a flight attendant and three pilots on board. The bills were stamped, which meant that Cooper could be arrested in the event he wanted to use any of his illegal gains. The two headed towards the south. It was dark, and it was raining lightly. After 45 minutes, he dispatched the stewardess in charge of checking the cockpit, while he started to getting ready for the parachute. He tied the bag with the cash onto his own body. He then lowered the back set of stairs and, just above the dark forest of winter Portland then he jumped off. After landing at the airport, all that was discovered were two parachutes left as well as an empty seat and the black tie.

The investigation

When the hijacked aircraft left the airport the authorities scrambled planes as well as helicopters to locate the plane. They were unable to locate Cooper's departure from the plane as they followed the hijacked aircraft to Seattle. The next few days the military commanded the sweeping of a thousand soldiers over the area in which Cooper is believed to had arrived. One way of investigating was flying the plane's original model across the ocean, and then throwing objects that resembled man's bodies at the door of the plane. Utilizing this method, investigators wanted to know the exact path Cooper took when he left the plane, and also to understand their pursuit for the man in the woods, however but in vain. Even the highly classified SR-71 Blackbird spy plane was employed to capture the forest in order to discover any trace of Cooper. They didn't find anything.

The investigation lasted for several years. In the year 1980, near the in the middle of the Columbia River, three bundles of cash were found in the hands of Brian Ingram, a boy who was constructing the foundation for a campfire in the area known as Tena Bar. Just a few inches beneath in the snow were the three bundles that were adorned with elastic bands. Since the serial numbers were identical to the notes marked by Cooper for $5,800 The FBI began to clean the area. They examined the river bed and dredged the river. Then, they found nothing.

As recently as 2007 the FBI was prepared to leave the investigation with the Special Agent Larry Carr, providing he was able to keep the cost and time to the minimal. Carr's method of detecting the hijacking in the same way as he would take on a bank robbery, talking about the incident with as many of the general public as he could. Although he was able discover a number of new pieces of details, there is no trace of the person or the rest of the cash.

Update

For many Americans the story in the case of Dan Cooper has now passed into legend. The man who disappeared and his money are treated that is similar to bank robbers of the previous west, their fame lasting. Due to this, the investigation into his crimes is now a pastime as well as an interest of numerous people. For them the matter rests on a few key questions.

The first question is the question of whether Cooper was killed when he jumped off the plane. Since no body was found and no one was ever found with money, it's difficult to determine if the suspect is dead. In the event of a skydivers with varying experiences have said that he was facing a tough scenario. For the beginner there was a risk of death. For experienced sky divers however, safety can be achieved. When he was removed from the plane and landing in the freezing cold, it may have hindered the chances of survival, but the body was never found. If you are debating the issue of Cooper's level of experience and his ability to use both back and front parachutes indicates that he was an amateur jumper. The refusal to allow anyone to teach him about how to leap indicates that he was confident enough in his own capabilities. The fact that he opted to use a parachute that was not able to steer indicates that he has a lower chance of survival, and also an inexperienced jumper, however, the description by the stewardess of him applying the parachute appears to suggest a competent man.

For some, the discovery of the cash seized by Brian Ingram adds complexion to the tale. 20 miles away from the place where the money rests lies the city of Ariel in the exact location an study on the zone of drop suggested Cooper could be. Some believe that the money was been swept away by a smaller set of rivers before arriving near Tena Bar. Another theory is that Cooper ended up on Tena Bar and needed to place his money there to avoid the pursuit of the FBI. The most bizarre of all is the idea of someone burying only a few bill notes to divert the authorities away from the false trail.

The other investigation is known by the name of Palmer Report and was commissioned by the FBI to conduct an analysis of the sandbar where the cash was discovered. Between an incident, and discovery of the cash in it was discovered that the Columbia River was dredged, and other sand was moved to Tena Var. In the Palmer Report found that the money was discovered in the upper layer of sand, which was dumped prior to the dredging. This is why it is possible to conclude that the money had been elsewhere until it was found at this spot. People who deny this idea draw attention to the fact it is true that these rubber bands did not disappear despite their sluggishness.

The flight's route is even being doubted. The original path map that can be found in the archive of the FBI does not provide any information on the process or date it was made. The map as drawn is believed to be a result of a thorough examination of flight data and flight recordings taken from radar sites. This particular path is an unintentional direction that does not contain Tena Bar or anywhere near the suspected locations. Due to this, the confusion regarding the possible loss of the funds is even difficult to identify and measure. Finding out how Cooper's money was swept away by the FBI flight route isn't easy. The issue of how three different bundles of marked notes managed to be separated from the remainder of the ransom remains difficult to determine. It is possible that the bag provided by the bank secured the money for a long time until it began to crumble, or Cooper lost the money in the jump or landing. It could be even possible that they were later buried by someone else at the time of his death to avoid a misdirection.

In contrast to other cases of missing persons one of the most interesting aspects of the Dan Cooper case Dan Cooper is that we do not know the identity of his previous. It is possible that he was in the region, which would allow him to distinguish the area from above. The mention of him as seeking "negotiable American currency" suggests that he might not be from America. Over the past several years searching for D. B. Cooper remains among the top notorious cases of missing persons. This is a mystery that will never be solved.

The man next door just vanished without prior warning.
The Who Zebb Quinn
Date it was: January 2 in 2000.
Location: Asheville, North Carolina
Context

In contrast to the case that was the case of D. B. Cooper and the other cases, not every case of disappearing persons is an intimate adventure or an unsolved crime. In some cases the horrifying human impact of the incident is enough to show that a disappearance is a truly bizarre emotional, sad, and demanding. The case for Zebb Quinn, the disappearance is an example of this.

That day

At the time of the celebration Zebb Quinn was working at Walmart. He met with a colleague in the huge car park approximately 9:00 in the afternoon. The two drove separate ways to meet with the seller of a car that Zebbb was looking to purchase. They were caught on CCTV footage fifteen minutes after. The friend, Robert Owens, would later inform police that on their drive, Quinn had signaled with his headlight to the two to stop. After that, Quinn informed his friend that he was being called and required to get to a telephone. After he rang the nearby payphone, Owens describes Quinn as being "frantic," and that the plans of theirs had to be canceled. In an eagle-like speed, Quinn ran his car into Owens's car.

It was the final time Quinn was observed.

A few hours later, Owens would get into another car crash and was required to undergo medical attention at an area hospital for fractured ribs. No investigation was filed by police in relation to this second crash.

The following day, Quinn's mother registered her missing person's claim.

The investigation

Prior to the investigation beginning with a seriousness at the time, the Walmart in which Quinn worked was contacted by a call from someone whom they claimed that they were Zebb Quinn. The caller informed the company that he was not able to work on that day because of illness. The employee who took the call was familiar with Quinn and recognized his voice. He reported his suspicions to the police. After tracing the call, they discovered that it came from the Volvo manufacturing plant, which was the one where Owens had been employed. After being interrogated, Owens said he was doing his friend a favor after being requested to do it from Quinn himself. Owens was not involved in the disappearance, however he was believed by the authorities as a person of concern.

The authorities began questioning acquaintances, including Quinn's love interest who was named Misty. They had a relationship during the time leading up to his disappearance and Zebb had advised family members and friends of their connection. Zebb had also told the public that her boyfriend one named Wesley was abusive and had made menaces against Quinn. After speaking to the police they both Misty and Wesley have denied involvement in disappearance of Zebb Quinn.

When looking through the phone records that pertain to the matter the information that Quinn got while driving was from the residence of Ina Ustich the paternal aunt of his. The two was not much prior to this phone call however Ustich is not adamant about having made the phone call. She was able to recall having dinner with a woman whose name was Tamara and was, in turn, Misty's mother. At the table included Misty as well as Wesley. The police investigation was initiated on an earlier date by Ustich who claimed that her house was broken into in the night in the incident. Although no evidence was found to suggest that the home had been taken, several photograph frames were taken.

After a fortnight of Zebb Quinn's disappearance Zebb Quinn, the car was found abandoned in the lot of the hospital, which was the same one where his mother worked. The car was discovered with a pair of lips traced across the rear of the vehicle and a sleeping puppy in the car. In addition the hotel card , however investigators were unable to find the establishment where it was utilized. The coat (not Quinn's) as well as several water bottles were found on the floor of the vehicle. The items was found to be any evidence from forensic analysis. The dog has been adopted by one the investigators. Quinn's mother believes that the location of the vehicle was planned and the perpetrator hoped that she would be able to find the car.

Update

Investigators haven't been able to find a suspect, however they have come to a variety of conclusions. They believe that several people were associated with the murder of Zebb Quinn, and that he was killed in the course that the crime took place. In addition the police have not been able to connect Owens, Misty, or Wesley to the investigation.

In the year 2015 Owens had been arrested for a separate case. Owens was believed to be in the case of the disappearance and death of Christie Schoen Codd, best known as a contestant of the Food Network show, as along with the disappearance of husband Joseph and their unborn child.

The story of a woman kidnapped by Bigfoot!
who: Theresa Bier
Date: 1 June 1987
Location: Fresno County, California
Context
We've covered the instances where people deliberately disappear and then disappear with no trace however what happens if the proposed theory seems extravagant? In the case that of

Theresa Bier, the explanation for her disappearance gained an enormous amount of attention than the fact that she vanished herself. To comprehend the circumstances it is essential to learn about the local mythology which surrounds her home town.

Native American tribes have long been telling stories about giants with hair who walked the forest since the time humans can remember. Once people from outside of the country came in and the tales started to be told. The creature came under various names. It doesn't matter if you call it Bigfoot, the Sasquatch, Bigfoot, or just a legend the mythology about the beast is well-known to many around the world. Many believe that the creatures traded with native tribes, and others claim that the creatures abducted children at night, or that they would kidnap women to find to find a potential partner. Whichever you choose to believe, it's this myth that has become inextricably connected with Theresa Bier.

On the same day

At the age of sixteen, Theresa Ann Bier ventured to camp in her State of California.

Alongside a year-old Russell "Skip" Welsh, their trip to 1987 led them towards the Central Sierras, allegedly in search of the monster that is known as Bigfoot. A few days later, Welch returned to the town with a compelling story. He initially told authorities that the girl had simply escaped from him. Then, he altered his story but he claimed that there was a Bigfoot was behind the kidnapping of Theresa.

The investigation

Authorities tried to accuse Welch with the kidnapping of Theresa Bier that year, however, they were unable present enough evidence to warrant that a conviction was given. One of the main issues was the absence of a corpse. Police believed that the discovery of Theresa could provide the proof they needed. They searched all over the region, including the area called Shuteye Peak, but could not locate any sign of a body.

Update

In a state of denial, unable to find the evidence required authorities were unable to find the evidence they needed from accusing Welch with abduction or murder. They still have hopes of finding an unidentified body, perhaps thirty years later. So, a trip to the site of the local area will give the public an address and phone number for contacting the department concerned with any information they may have. Without such proof and with just Welch's claim that Bigfoot is responsible We may never be able to know the truth that led to the mysterious disappearance of Theresa Bier. While it's not as likely as his theory may seem, his assertion of Bigfoot's involvement has elevated this mystery from a simple disappearance to the realm of the supernatural.

The wild human rights lawyer and author who disappeared in Mexico
The person: Oscar Zeta Acosta
When: May, 1974
The location: Mazatlan, Mexico
Context
The way that people are remembered following their disappearance is often a factor in the way

we look at the case the case. In the case of Oscar Acosta, the fame earned through his connection in the company of Hunter S. Thompson proved to be a long-lasting tribute to his worldview that was a reflection of his.

The story of Acosta's starts with the town in El Paso, Texas. Acosta was the son of an Mexican immigrants as well as an American woman, Oscar was their third child, but the only one who lived. He was born in California close to his hometown of Modesto. His father was drafted during the Second World War. This was the path Acosta was to follow when he joined in the Air Force after graduating high school. He was released a few days after that and then returned to school initially at an institution in the local area, and later at San Francisco State University. He merged his love of creative writing and an education in law from evening school. He passed the bar exam in 1966. He worked for a number of years to end the poverty of Oakland.

Then, he relocated into Los Angeles and proceeded to establish a name for himself with LAPD. LAPD (Los Los Angeles Police

Department) through his work as an activist lawyer for various groups, including those of the Chicano 13 and the Brown Berets. As a result his work, he was frequently targeted and threatened by law enforcement officials in the area. There was even a connection to a mysterious group called The Chicano Liberation Front, who claimed to be responsible for a string of bombings throughout the state. At the attention of officers and FBI the next step was in his bid to become Sheriff of Los Angeles County, receiving 100,000 votes. In the course of his campaign the candidate was forced to spend a few days in prison after being found guilty of infractions to the law. He was defeated in the election - his opponent received more than one million votes, but managed to beat his local rival, Everett Holladay, the Chief of Police in Monterey Park.

Acosta published his first novel in 1972. It was entitled Autobiography of the Brown Buffalo. The story was based upon the life of a lawyer who fights for the rights of those who were disadvantaged by the society. The author followed it up with his next major work, The

Revolt of the Cockroach People. Through his writing and fame resulting in his rise to a status of a public persona, and his close relationship with the famous Hunter S. Thompson, the abrupt departure of Acosta was so shocking that it was to be fitting.

That day

In the month of May 1974 Acosta traveled to Mexico. He made a final message to child Marco from Mazatlan the final destination. He informed his son that he planned to "board the boat that was stuffed with fluffy white snow." The call was never heard from for the rest of his life. In a conversation in the future, Marco provides the following idea about what transpired in the presence of his father "We believe that it was likely due to the people he was associated with and the people he was with, he ended up yelling off, getting in an argument, and eventually being killed."

The investigation

Since he disappeared in Mexico In addition to the reputation of Acosta Due to his reputation, the FBI along with the American police were not able (or indifferent) to conduct an investigation.

However, this doesn't mean that the investigation could not be completed however, with the assistance of a good acquaintance Hunter S. Thompson conducting his own research in the form of an article which would later appear on Rolling Stone. It was entitled "The Banshee Screams for Buffalo Meat" and published on the 27th of July, 1977. Thompson states Acosta as an effective attorney and a person who preached his beliefs, but was hampered by an increase in amphetamines. Additionally, Acosta has a known habit of using LSD. As per Thompson, Acosta was either killed by a group of drug dealers or been killed to protect political motives. In addition to Thompson other people have claimed that a drug overdose or a mental breakdown could cause the disappearance of Acosta.

Update

One possible scenario proposed by Thompson suggested that Acosta could still be in good health after having fled Miami to avoid the attention of his adversaries. In spite of speculation and rumours about the truth, the speculation about his death has led to his tale becoming increasingly complicated and complex. In the wake of representations in films like Fear and Loathing in Las Vegas, Acosta and Thompson have become icons of the counterculture. In contrast to Thompson (who later committed suicide) Acosta's status being a person who is missing contributes to his fame. In his eulogy of "one of God's most famous models," Thompson has helped to create a popular image of Acosta that continues to be cherished until today. Although we will never be able to determine what actually happened or the exact location of his departure however, the manner the way his memory is being preserved by relatives and friends has ensured that he won't be overlooked.

The first American missing person

Who is: Virginia Dare

When: 1587-1590

Where: Virginia Colony, North Carolina

The baptism of Virginia Dare, lithography by Henry Howe, 1876

Context

A large number of Americans disappear into thin air and disappear into the night, but this is not an uncommon phenomenon. While some blame Bigfoot or drugs, some are blamed on Bigfoot and others on murder, the tradition of people disappearing has been a part of America since the time that Europeans first came here. Perhaps the most reliable evidence for this fact is the history of Virginia Dare. First Caucasian who was born within the British colonies of North America, Virginia was born in the Roanoke Colony in 1587. Because of the age at the birth, little information is available about the parents of her. The mother of her was colony's governor , and had been birthed in London. She was married to a bricklayer called Ananias in London in the church of Fleet Street. The couple enlisted in the Roanoke expedition and travelled into an unknown land. Virginia was the only of two kids born to colonists in 1587 , and the only girl.

We know only a tiny quantity about the life of Virginia Dare due to the end that was the Roanoke Colony. The colony's founding father, John White - Virginia's great-grandfather - set sail to England in 1587 in order to get new supplies. In that time England had been engaged in an ongoing war with Spain. This resulted in huge demand for ships. This made it impossible for him to return in America up to 1590. In 1590, Virginia would have been three years old. When she arrived at Roanoke Colony it was discovered to be abandoned for years. The structures had begun to decay and the homes of inhabitants had collapsed into decay. White could not find any trace of his familymembers; none of his son-in-law, daughter-in-law or his young granddaughter. It was impossible to locate the 80 people who lived in the colony, nor of the 17 women or 11 children. It was later called The Lost Colony.

That day

It is believed that the disappearance of Virginia Dare and her family remains an unsolved mystery. There are theories suggested as to what may have occurred during the period when John White was away. There was no evidence to suggest that battle or fighting occurred on the spot, with detectives locating that the term "croatoan" cut into the fort of the settlers. This word "cro" was written on the stump of a tree discovered close to the settlement. As the colony was leaving it was given in the hands of White to ensure that the cross be cut into the nearby tree to signify the danger. Without a cross, White believed that the colonists were moving to close Croatoan Island, which is now called Hatteras Island. All in all, only a few evidence was discovered which left historians of the present to provide theories in the future.

The investigation

The most commonly accepted theory is that colonists encountered a tribe in the area and sought refuge with these neighbors. Thereafter, they could have had a relationship or even fought. Another colony known as the Jamestown Colony of 1607 - began to look for information about their lost predecessors. One of the suggestions they received was a story of the local Chesapeake Indians. Their chief had an alternative story to those of colonists seeking refuge, saying that they were fighting and killing the earliest colonists. The one of the Jamestown colonists James Smith, was allowed to look at artefacts as well as belongings were claimed to belong to Roanoke colonists. The items included a musket and a mortar, but nothing has been found to this day. The Jamestown colonists set out in search of additional information or survivors, but they found nothing. So, all the colonists were assumed to be dead.

Update

The story has continued to be a fascination for historians. In a book published in 2000, Lee Miller added weight to the idea it was the Roanoke colonists sought refuge from those of the Chowanoc tribe. The clan was later attacked by a separate tribe, called the Mandoag but the evidence suggests that the tribe could be called The Wainoke as well as Tiscarora. The incident was described in a more detailed way, William Strachey was a secretary for the colony later located in Jamestown. He had a record of two grand homes as parts of Indian settlements in Peccarecanick and Ochanahoen and Ochanahoen, which had stone walls that were unlike anything else that the natives were familiar with they allegedly learned the techniques from Roanoke colonists. He also records a variety of reports of captures of Europeans in the same time and includes the four Englishmen along with children. The captives were forced to work by beating and making copper. The captive Europeans, Strachey reports, were able to escape attack on another colony and had fledbefore arriving in the present-day North Carolina.

From all of the pioneers that vanished Of all the settlers who disappeared, it's Virginia Dare who has become the most well-known. She has become a recognizable character in many American myths and stories and has been a symbol of many virtues because of her age and innocence. She is now a symbol of an attitude of courage and adventure, and was one of the first people to be born in a new country that later became the home of her family. Through the ages, various North Carolina political groups have employed her to symbolize the importance of the rights of European-Americans in the beginning of the Twentieth Century. There is even a contemporary anti-immigration organization uses her name to describe their organization which is named VDARE Project. VDARE Project.

In addition to her political significance There is also an honorary memorial for Virginia Dare in Saint Bride's Church located on Fleet Street in London. It is home to the bronze and marble statue and the latter is missing since 1999. Despite modern versions of the story being distorted and used for various reasons of ideology in the midst of the story is a small girl who was reported missing. Being one of the newest missing people in the book (and also one of the oldest cases) the story of her disappearance is an example of how that the possibility of someone missing is not just a matter of time.

CHAPTER 2: A HORROR AUTHOR WHO DISAPPEARED INTO THE DARKNESS

Person: Ambrose Bierce

When: 1914

Where: Chihuahua, Chihuahua, Mexico

Context

For a few of those missing who have been missing, their skepticism and dark views of life have been reflected in their disappearing finals. In the case of Ambrose Pierce in the early Twentieth Century, his fame as a snarky author and journalist, along with his interest in and the Mexican Revolution, cast a shadow over his disappearance.

Ambrose Gwinnett Bierce was born on June 24, 1842. In his professional life as an editor, a writer as well as a satirist, visionary and an agnostic. The story he wrote "An Oddity of the Owl Creek Bridge" has become one of the most known works of American literature. His brutal critiques of various artistic endeavors could best be illustrated in the phrase that became an euphemism to Bierce; "nothing matters." His dark view of the work of men led to earn him his nickname, Bitter Bierce.

His distinct style of writing could be seen in both his journalistic work and creative writing with a frequent sudden start, before settling into dark images, and later returning to the theme of war. It was his obsession of war, which was to ultimately cause his disappearance.

That day

Aged 71 in the month of October 1913 Bierce quit his residence in Washington and set off on an exploration of the historical Civil War battle sites. He traveled through southern states including Louisiana and Texas and finally, he reached El Paso and crossing the border to Mexico. The country was at the midst of a revolutionary movement and the events of that revolution motivated him to join the army of Pancho Villa as an observer. In the same position that he saw the fight at Tierra Blanca.

After joining Villa's army, Bierce is known to travel to Chihuahua and left his last message to the world by writing an email to his friend Blanche Partington. The letter was composed the day following Christmas 1913. The letter was closed informing his friend the letter was sent to unspecified destinations. Following that, he disappeared. From all the entries in the timeless literary canon that is American literature His disappearance in the present is among the most well-known.

According to the stories that were passed down via word-of-mouth and recorded in the writings of James Lienert, a priest, Bierce was sentenced to execution by firing squad in the town's cemetery in Sierra Mojada, Coahuila. The story is not entirely confirmed but there are a variety of biographers suggesting that Bierce might not have been able to ride because of his asthmatic condition and being extremely negative about Pancho Villa previously. Such criticisms can only increase the mystery surrounding the disappearance of Bierce, and some are unsure if Bierce even traveled to Mexico in the first place.

The investigation

Although there have been numerous investigations into the circumstances of Ambrose Bierce, they have offered only a few information. There is no evidence to suggest that he went to Mexico but there is also no proof that he didn't. The theories that range from suicide to firing squads have been offered however none of them have the essential evidence required for the making of a definitive decision.

Update

The topic of Bierce's disappearance has become a hot topic for filmmakers and writers. The Old Gringo is a novel written by Carlos Fuentes that has also been made into a movie featuring Gregory Peck. Bierce's disappearance as well as his experiences within Mexico are the focus of the movie and novel, with the tale being told in the"From Dusk Till Dawn 3," the sequel to the vampire novel "From Dusk Till Dawn 3." In addition to this, a lot of Bierce's works are being adapted for screenplays, helping in bringing his tale to the new generation of viewers.

According to one biographer, the existence of Bierce's twisted attitude was further exacerbated due to his involvement with his participation in the Mexican Civil War. It's the notion that "nothing is important" that has always affected the demise of Bitter Bierce. From those who called the genius of his work to those who were enraged by his sardonicity The writer's disappearance, as well as the mysterious circumstances that surround it are always influenced by the persona of Bierce as a person.

America's most well-known missing person
Who is: Charles Augustus Lindbergh Jr.
The date: March 1, 1932
Location: East Amwell, New Jersey
The context: Of of the disappearances throughout American history Perhaps the most well-known was the one from the Lindbergh baby. The son of famous icons The kidnapping triggered national searches and a tale that is passed down to the present. It was and remains among the top reported criminal incidents in the last 100 years. Regarding what it teaches us

about past of missing people and the way in which they disappear, it's an illustration of how public support can surround a crime and the ways in which the media can be caught into the mystery of the disappearance of the person.

If you're not familiar with the tale The grandparents of Charles Lindbergh, Jr were famous pilots. They were known for their accomplishments and flying capabilities, the couple had already been one of the nation's most famous couples, appearing in national newspapers and interacting with the elite of society. On the 1st day of March 1932, the lives of these two were to change forever.

That day

At 8 p.m. in the evening of March 1, Betty Gow threw the baby to the bed. As the nurse in the family she knew the 20-month old baby just as everyone else. She put him on the blanket and secured it with pins to keep the baby from moving throughout his sleeping. After an hour and a half later, the boy's dad, Charles Lindbergh Sr thought that he heard something outside. He thought that it was the fall of wooden slats that had fallen from an old crate.

When he returned home at 10pm, Betty returned to examine the baby, she noticed that he had not been asleep in his bed. After asking the parents of the child they examined themselves and find the exact same issue. The baby Charles was absent.

With his gun in hand, Charles Sr searched the home for any signs of intrusion. The local police were summoned in addition to the media as well as the lawyer that represented the family. A single tire footprint was to be found in the dirt, and made evident by the rain that fell during the day. In a quick search, the police found three pieces of an unfinished ladder hidden in the nearby bush. The ladder was well-constructed, but it was built in a straightforward manner. The baby had gone.

The investigation

After the news broke, story following the news, the Lindberghs were bombarded with messages and requests for assistance and assistance. The responses included a variety of false information. The offers came from gangsters like Al Capone, who sent his plea from inside a prison cell. While investigators searched both high and low in search of the missing child three days of searching turned into nothing. The kidnappers did not speak to the kidnappers until a letter was delivered, with a request for $70,000. After further discussions and discussion, the kidnappers outlined their plan for how the money would be handed over. Following their plan the kidnappers stated it was possible that Lindbergh baby could be located on the Nelly which is a vessel in Massachusetts. After the authorities looked around, they could not find anything. They could not locate the child and the boat, but it didn't appear to be there. Then the most terrifying nightmare of the Lindbergs was realized. Baby Charles's body was discovered close to their mansion, had been murdered during the night of his disappearance. It was located just a mile away from their house The Lindberghs realized they were no longer able to live there and decided to donate the house to a foundation for charitable purposes.

It appeared that the case was unsolvable. continued to be open for two years two years later. In the fall of 1934 one of the marked-up bills from the ransom was found. It was found at a station and discovered by an attendant who took note of an license plate for the vehicle after becoming concerned about the driver. The clue was traced to Bruno Hauptmann, a German Immigrant. After a thorough inspection of his residence investigators found a stash of ransom money.

The money, according to Hauptmann was handed the money by his relative who asked that keep it. Hauptmann claimed that he had no connection with the kidnapping. However, the trial that followed quickly was the subject of media's investigation. In spite of the absence of evidence to support the German handwriting experts provided evidence linking the ransom note with Hauptmann's hand. In conjunction with the engraved bills, and even the kind of wood used to construct the ladder and the ladder, the evidence was sufficient to prove that Hauptmann was guilty. Due to the crime, kidnapping was eventually be a federal crime. Mainmann's execution was scheduled for the following day.

Update

In spite of the verdict however, there is still a debate regarding whether Bruno Hauptmann is guilty. Still, there are questions regarding the manner in which it was solved as well as the possibility that the trial was fair. There have been rumors that evidence was fabricated or altered and that the widow of Hauptmann was being able to sue authorities in the state of New Jersey on two occasions and claiming that the execution was unjust of Bruno. Each time the lawsuit was dismissed.

Escapees from America's harshest prison who have never wanted to be discovered

Who are: Frank Morris and John and Clarence Anglin

Date: 11 June 1962

Location: Alcatraz Island, San Francisco, California

Context

While certain criminals have led to the disappearances of others and others have gone missing themselves. We've previously reported that disappearances of D. B. Cooper led to some of the biggest and most well-known instances of missing persons in American history. However, there have been occasions that the disappearance has occurred after the verdict. With regard to Frank Morris and the Anglin Brothers their status as missing persons is a matter of escape.

The prison island of Alcatraz was frequently regarded to be one of most difficult prisons. The prisoners who managed to escape did not just have to contend with guards and walls and the prison, but also had to navigate through the turbulent waters around the prison. If they did escape and were later found to be an unidentified person could be a sign that they escaped from the prison or lost their lives trying. In this instance the escapees never discovered.

In the years prior to their prison sentence As a prelude to their detention, they were sentenced to prison. Anglin brothers (Clarence and John) were a couple from Georgia who left their work as laborers in order to take over banks. Their robbery career was not very last long as it ended in their arrest and sentenced in 1956. After attempting to escape from Atlanta State Penitentiary, the brothers were taken to the toughest prison in America, Alcatraz. They arrived a year apart and soon being allowed to catch up with their former acquaintance, Frank Morris, whom they had met at another prison.

Frank Morris was born in Washington and spent a large part of his childhood in various foster care facilities and in homes. As an orphan at the age of 11, he was convicted of his first crime at the age of 13. His crimes of occurrence range from robbery and drug-related crimes to narcotic offenses. Similar to the other brothers, he unsuccessfully attempted to escape Atlanta and was taken to Alcatraz. Alcatraz in the year 1960 as part of a sentence lasting 14 years. In the face of a difficult prison time The group decided to flee.

That day

The plan was to be executed on the 11th of June on the 11th of June, 1962, in the darkness of the night. The group had created representations of themselves with the mixture of soap, toilet paper as well as bits and pieces of actual hair. They were put inside their cells to fool guards into believing that they were sleeping. They were using spoons to make hole through the walls of their cells. They had to wait for an entire year. In their cell they were escorted to an open corridor for service leaving four prisoners behind, one of whom could not get out of his cell.

In the corridor they were not using and a vent, they walked up and climbed up the shaft until they reached the roof. The loud sound was ignored by the guards, who believed the noise to be not too serious. The three men began their descent from the tops roofs, and then climbed the wall that surrounded the prison. They then built an adobe raft with cement that resembles glue and typical prison raincoats. They then inflated their creations as they sat on the north-easterly portion of the island. Just two hours before midnight, they plunged into the water and started trying to get to the shore. The investigation

In the jail the disappearance of the prisoners was not discovered until the following day. The false heads were at work. After conducting a thorough sweep across the entire island security guards and police did not find any evidence of the Anglins. However, they did discover a few traces of the raft as well as its paddles as well in a bag that held some of the personal belongings of Anglin. The debris was been found on the shores of an island nearby.

According to the FBI they believed it was feasible for the suspects to make it to the adjacent Angel Island, but the frigid water they had to cross as well as the direction of the tide at the moment they left resulted in it being extremely unlikely. Additionally, they questioned the prisoner that was abandoned. He told the authorities that the idea was to rob an automobile and disguises when arriving at their destination, but the items were ever reported missing. Due to this, the FBI decided to end their investigation in 1979 in the belief that the prisoners suffered an unlucky fate in the water, drowning in cold water in their attempt to find their freedom. With no bodies, however the issue of missing prisoners remains an issue of debate. U.S. Marshalls have maintained warrants for the arrest of the accused, should they come to light.

Update

Due to how the escape occurred as well as the fame that has been attached to Alcatraz as "the inexplicably confined jail," many have tried to imagine what the group might have done to been able to escape. One of these investigations was conducted by the popular TV program "MythBusters." It was on the Discovery Channel program began to explore the possibility of the escape plan by testing rafts against waters and the tide. While they concurred that with FBI in that they wouldn't not have been able get to Angel Island, they suggested that a trip to Marin Headlands could be possible.

A few years after the initial incident, an individual called Bud Morris - a cousin of Frank claimed to have delivered sealed envelopes to some individuals who were Alcatraz guards. In 2011 at the age of 89, he also claimed that he had spoken to his cousin for a brief period of time following the apparently successful escape attempt. To support this claim Bud Morris's daughter who was aged eight or nine and who was at the time of the meeting along with his cousin "Uncle Frank." At the time, she was aware of little about the escape and says she knows nothing later on.

To this to this, the 50th anniversary of the tragedy saw the remaining sister of the Anglins come forward to say that they believed that John and Clarence were alive. In addition, they also reaffirmed their belief that the brothers are still alive to this day, and then in 2012. They also recalled the phone call of John just after the escape , and an unopened Christmas card sent to the family by John the year 1962.

Despite family members' claims regarding the prisoner's survival it is possible that we will not know the fate of the prisoners. If they came forward today, they'd be nearing the age of 100 and could have died of natural causes following a lifetime of fugitive status. As is the case in America the fascination of the criminals who may be successful ensures that their stories will continue to remain in the past regardless of the theories or evidence presented. When it comes to missing persons they are definitely the ones who want to remain undiscovered in case they are found guilty of a repeat offense.

Who can locate a person when the police themselves are the main suspects?

The Who's: Terrance Williams and Felipe Santos

Date when: October 1, 2003/January 12 in 2004

The location: Naples, Florida

Context

If there's one factor you'd like to be able to count on in a missing person investigation, it's the police. However, in this case the institution we trust to protect us is the one that suspects could be the cause for the incident. Terrance Williams as well as Felipe Santos have been missing for more than 10 years. Although they disappeared months apart and a striking resemblance between their cases suggest the involvement of dark forces. Although neither of them was charming, the circumstances the circumstances in which they disappeared are far from improbable. To get the most accurate information it is necessary to look at the events themselves.

On the same day

The first part of this article will focus on the tale of Felipe Santos. Santos was an illegal Mexican who was living in Florida illegally. Santos had been living in the United States for three years with no legal documents. He sent money back regularly to help the family which he abandoned in his home country. The last time anyone was able to see him alive was on October 1 of 2003 at about half past seven in the early morning. Along with two brother's, Felipe was in his vehicle and headed to work. The trio was involved in an accident of a minor nature during their drive through Naples and prompted the local Sheriff's deputy Steve Calkins to give him an citation for a variety of traffic offenses, including driving without a permit or insurance on the car, as well as reckless driving. After being issued a citation, Santos was placed into the vehicle of the patrol.

Santos is the final time that his siblings saw Santos.

When he heard that Santos was detained and his boss called an area jail for him to set an employee's bail but was shocked to learn they did not have a evidence of an arrest. When confronted by Calkins about the incident the officer said that he'd had an alteration of mind and took the decision to let his prisoner go at the local store before taking off. This explanation appeared to be in contradiction to the story of the other party involved in the traffic collision and said that the law enforcement officer was "agitated" by the incident because Santos was not carrying the proper documents.

Then, it required Calkins about two weeks write an account of the incident. Following this, the family of Santos filed a missing persons' investigation, along with an accusation against the officer who was arrested. After a quick review, Calkins was cleared of any infractions. Felipe Santos, however, hasn't been seen since then, triggering critiques from his wife who claims that she hasn't even been questioned about the incident.

A few months later, Terrance Williams vanished under similar circumstances. Like Santos, Williams was an American citizen. The date was January 12, 2004. Williams was on his own when he disappeared. The only person who had communication with Williams was his roommate named Jason Gonzalez, who was in contact with him in the late evening. Williams was invited to a work-related party and was on his way home to get ready for the day's work. He wasn't legally licensed and had a valid and valid driver's licence, being previously cited for driving while impaired. In addition the registration for his vehicle was due to expire. In a state of confusion, unable to figure out a way to get there so he decided to travel legally. When he didn't come to home that evening, his roommate was worried. He sent an email to Terrance Williams's mom about his disappearance. Terrance was never ever seen again.

The investigation

It was reported that the disappearance of Terrance Williams was reported shortly after the missing persons report was submitted. Instead of police, however Terrance's aunt was the one who first discovered her nephew's car, after it was towed away from the graveyard in Naples. The tower's report indicated that the vehicle stopped traffic and was completed by Steve Calkins. When the family called the police they quickly found out that Calkins had not filed a formal reports of the incident, nor did he make an arrest.

The family of Terrance further investigated. His mother contacted the workers at the cemetery and found out via them Calkins actually pulled the vehicle over and demanded the driver to provide identification. He was the driver Terrance Williams did not have such documents. The cemetery workers were able to recall being witness to the deputy rubbing the suspect, who was later tucked into behind the vehicle of police. People who worked in the cemetery on that day were also aware of the policeman soliciting permission to let the vehicle that was causing trouble at the cemetery parking area. He left along with Terrance Williams sitting in the rear of the vehicle. After a short while workers recollect Calkins returning to the scene, and then moving Terrance's Cadillac to the opposite direction and putting keys lying on the ground close to the vehicle.

As suspicions grew The Williams family started to report reports to police. They would call the station frequently and asked to speak with Calkins. The station then contacted Calkins themselves and requested additional details regarding the incident and the deputy denied there was no evidence of any cars tow in this way or even apprehension of anyone on that day.

Calkins' supervisors requested him to submit an account. The report covered the incident, noting that Calkins was able to stop Williams following a report that the young man was "in distressed." When he pulled the offender the deputy states that Williams demanded an excursion to a nearby shop, and he agreed. He was told that the right documents were in the vehicle however, when he returned to the car,

Calkins discovered that this wasn't the situation. He tried to find Williams but without success. Calkins looked deeper and discovered that the vehicle hadn't been registered and Williams was not working at the location like he had claimed. Police investigated the story of Calkins, but could not locate any evidence of corroborating footage from the CCTV or telephone. Store employees couldn't remember the incident, and there were no witnesses were found that were in agreement with Calkins. At this time, Terrance Williams's family lodged an official complaint with the deputy.

There was no other leads, and no evidence of foul or criminal activity - just one missing person. It was at this point the family of Terrance was approached by representatives from the Mexican Consulate in Miami to inform them of another case that involved the same police officer.

After it was determined that Calkins was implicated in multiple incident, the investigation was made more complicated. Police officers scrutinized the conversations he had with dispatchers recordings, and they revealed some differences in the accounts. Calkins was heard to describe the vehicle as abandoned and an obstruction to the thoroughfare. The witness accounts were in contradiction and the statement of Calkins himself. Police were unsure of what to consider. Calkins could be heard laughing regarding the possible scenario that an "abandoned vehicle" owner might find themselves in the graveyard but then come back to discover that their car is missing. Also, there was language that implied racism in the possible owners of the Cadillac. After just twenty minutes of the meeting, the deputy demanded information about the background of Terrance Williams. This was in direct contradiction to Calkins claim that he did never even heard the person's last name. Calkins when questioned on the subject, was unable to explain the contradictions. Then, he stopped to cooperate and was dismissed from the local police department. Two of the men, however were never found.

Update

Due to the nature of this case the larger law enforcement agencies were contacted to assist.

However neither authorities from the Florida Department of Law Enforcement or the FBI could provide further information. Despite the use of the use of tracking devices as well as forensic evidence techniques and sniffer dogs, nothing more evidence about the suspects was ever discovered. There has been no arrests and investigations have come to an abrupt halt. In some cases, the most suspect disappearances cannot be solved.

CHAPTER 3: A DISAPPEARANCE AN INDIVIDUAL WHO IS LOOKING FOR THE NEXT ADVENTURE

Who is Andrew McAuley?

When when: February 9, 2007

The location: Tasman Sea, Australia

Context

In many cases we observe that those who disappear are in mysterious and enigmatic circumstances. They may be performing something routine or in their everyday routine until they disappear completely ever again. Sometimes individuals may have intentionally sought to find hazardous and challenging situations and then disappeared. Although it does make their tales more tragic, instances like the one of Andrew McAuley could cause audiences to be confused and lost regarding the excitement that comes from these kinds of experiences.

born in the year 1968 Andrew McAuley was an adventurer from Australia. Andrew McAuley became known for his sea kayaking as well as his ascent of mountains in the most difficult locations around the world. It was this desire for thrills that led Andrew in danger in February 2007.

That day

We are not aware of the happenings that transpired during the day. Because of Andrew's journey and his attempt to go on a solo trip across a large body water. He was adrift and unaccompanied but was believed to be only eighty kilometers away from his dream location. He was trying to traverse the sea that runs between Australia in New Zealand. Although the idea of crossing the vast expanse of water could cause a skepticism among the majority of people, it didn't matter to Andrew. For Andrew the personal risk was enough to propel him into danger.

The only evidence that we have regarding the incidents of the day is one radio broadcast. The static-filled "garbled" signal was picked up by authorities they were unable to determine the exact meaning of what Andrew was trying to convey. The next day his kayak was discovered floating upside down. Andrew was not observed.

The investigation

The investigation into the disappearance of McAuley was initiated immediately. The coroner that investigated the case stated that the kayaker had the GPS tracker that he may be able to attach to his body, assisting authorities in their hunt. The discovery of such a device could provide more information about the distress call that was becoming increasingly alarming for friends and family members. The coroner also noted that Andrew used his radio to inform his location numerous occasions throughout the course of his day.

In the course of investigating, the coroner, Ms. Savage - did lodge an opinion about the apparent delay in the attempts to save Andrew. The delay was further aggravated because many believed that the distress message to be some kind of hoax. In reviewing the message that was received, the family members of Andrew McAuley were urged to only listen to a little of the message lest it turn into a disturbing. Without a body and not being able to locate the GPS tracker Andrew McAuley's body not found.

Update

Andrew's tale is both amazing and tragic. This is why filmmakers were inspired to create an documentary about Andrew's life. The documentary Solo named Solo: Lost at Sea is about the adventures of Andrew's voyage across Tasmania across the ocean to New Zealand. The documentary features footage of Andrew as well as of the waters that he tried to traverse, as well as interviews with associates who are known to him. If you are seeking more details about Andrew McAuley's disappearance Andrew McAuley, this film could provide a fascinating glimpse into the man who was a fugitive.

The brilliant computer scientist who disappeared without a trace

Jim Gray Jim Gray

Date: January 28th 2007, 2007

The location: San Francisco

Context

Of all the professions seem to be immune from mysterious disappearances and strange events computer scientists are one of the few professions that is least likely to be implicated. In the instance of Jim Grey, however, even an award like the Turing Award was not enough to stop him from disappearing. Since he's been declared dead it is possible to examine his past and see if it is possible to use it to warn other people who could be susceptible to similar situations.

James "Jim" Gray was born in 1944. He was recognized for his work that advanced the field of computer science. Particularly his work in the field of database and transaction processing was described as seminal , and has resulted in technological leadership in the area that of system integration.

From California Jim's mother worked as an educator and his father served serving in the Army. When Jim was a young child the family relocated to Rome. Jim spent a lot of his life speaking Italian as his first language. Then, they returned to America initially to Virginia and later to San Francisco after the divorce of Jim's parents. The father of Jim even managed to patent a specific design for ribbons for typewriters that brought the family a large royalty.

Looking to join the Air Force, Jim was rejected. He decided instead to attend at the University of California at Berkley. To finance his studies, he started working for General Dynamics in a position that helped him learn the intricate details and complexities of Monroe Calculator. Monroe calculator. After a period of six months off from studying and a return to school, he returned and finished studying Engineering Mathematics. From there, Jim married and took an employment within New Jersey, in Bell Labs. In the beginning, they planned to earn enough money to take a trip for 5 years, Jim and his wife discovered their desire to travel satisfied after just two months from their jobs. Following this, Jim earned his PhD in programming languages, and began his research in the area in computer science.

With this exciting and vital job already in place, Jim became a keen sailing enthusiast. With a good life and a sedentary hobby, Jim began to partake in a few sailing trips. In 2007 Jim was planning a trip in San Francisco. San Francisco area.

On the same day

The day Jim chose for his excursion was a Saturday in January. The idea was to take a boat towards Farallon Island. Farallon Islands, which are situated close to. With the ashes of his mother, Jim wanted to scatter them at the exact location. Jim took his 40-foot boat out to sea , but was never ever seen again. Donna Jim's wife was the first to report him missing. The report triggered a massive search and rescue operation to discover what transpired to Jim's computer science professor.

The investigation

The initial actions of the Coast Guard were to transport helicopters, planes or patrol vessels to the location but did not discover any evidence. One clue was that the vessel was equipped by an emergency radio transmitter, a piece of equipment which is activated and broadcasts distress signals in the event that the vessel begins sinking. The location Jim chose was far enough from busy shipping routes that were which travel between San Francisco Bay. The weather was calm and there were no reports of collisions or sea-related collisions. There were no emergency radio broadcasts. Jim was missing in plain sight.

Authorities have partnered with an satellite to show photographs of the sea within the area. They were uploaded online and people started to flip between the huge number of photos. They came across nothing. Following the disappearance, , many wanted to offer theories of the circumstances. However, none of them were capable of providing a satisfactory explanation however. It was a few weeks before the family officially ended their search to find Jim. They continued to search for every possible clue, and even an underwater search that yielded no results. Jim was officially declared dead after being unaccounted for for since a long time.

Update

In recognition of the crucial and significant work done by Jim Gray, his memory is remembered by numerous important and renowned institutions. For instance, UC Berkeley held a tribute to their student in 2008 that included talks and discussions of Richard Rashid and David Vaskevitch. The tech giant Microsoft even committed its WorldWide Telescope program to Jim Gray to commemorate his accomplishments. Microsoft also established an research center named in honor of the missing computer scientist. It is unclear if it was suicide, accidental, or something else Jim Gray's disappearance Jim Gray is one instance which has left many puzzled.

When a disappearance gets wrapped in the past of a mysterious group of people who are a cult

Who: Michele Miscavige

When: August 2007,

Where the location is: Unknown

Context

In some of those cases that are most controversial published in this publication, the people who are accused or blamed with murder or kidnapping appear to be psychotic or crazy people or may have an motivation for their actions that is financial in nature. In this case the disappearance is believed to be the result of one of the world's most mysterious and most secretive movements. It is the Church of Scientology is no one to be averse to controversy, however the disappearance from the home of the group's leader has been frequently claimed to be among the most intriguing and troubling features of their ascendancy to the top of the pyramid. The attempts of this case to understand the disappearance of Michele Miscavige frequently result in trying to get through the unclear water of morality in the church.

Michele is born on the year 1961. The daughter was an old-time religious member in the sister group, Sea Org. In the year 1980, she was married to her co- Church members David and Mary Miscavige one of the men who will later be the head in Scientology. Scientology movement. The controversial religion has gained a reputation for the moral ambiguity of their practices and their litigious nature. In the middle of the debate is the way the Church treats its followers. Perhaps the most obvious example are the bizarre circumstances which have led to Michele's deportation from the public sphere.

On the same day

Decribing the day Michele disappeared can be difficult. Instead of an abrupt disappearance Michele was merely withdrawn from the public sphere, disappearing from any public gatherings she may have attended previously. Although she may have been present attending Church of Scientology events or out with her husband, she hasn't been seen in public since the month of August 2007. In lieu of putting a precise time frame for her disappearance Michele has merely stopped to appear to.

In 2006, her husband had left the base in the world for Scientology. Church of Scientology. At this point, Michele took on his post and started making several changes that were noticeable.

One of the major modifications was to stifle her husband's "special relation" that was forged with her husband Church members Tom Cruise. The changes included altering the schedule of the two to prevent any possibility of the two having a romantic time.

When David was back after his vacation, witnesses have reported Michele experiencing an "visible shift" in her attitude and appearance. When confronted about this shift, Church spokesperson Mike Rinder mentioned that Michele asked him if David was wearing the wedding ring he received. Then, a short time later she stopped appearing in public. She wasn't at the wedding ceremony of Tom Cruise, one of the largest Church occasions. 2013 was the year that a former church member, Leah Remini, reported receiving a lot of abuse during the wedding. She also mentioned that Michele did not attend the wedding.

According to the critics of The Church, the situation is because of how her husband acted as well as the Church. The Church itself has released statements have been made public that claim that Michele is working only to address the needs of the Church in private. They have not been able to reveal her whereabouts at any point. This led to the report of multiple missing persons reports. The reports were closed with authorities from the Los Angeles Police Department, they have described them as "unfounded," though no information about the incident was released. A detective involved in the case has claimed that they were permitted to have meetings with Michele at least a few times. In addition, few information exists regarding the location Michele could be.

The investigation

While investigating the case researchers have discovered that events that led to the disappearance of Michele may provide clues about her current situation. Although there are numerous reports of missing persons being filed, the results are classified and access to reports is not allowed. The reason for this is due to members of the police force claiming they have had meetings with Michele however these meetings aren't specific. The details about the investigation remain in the smatterings. Any speculations regarding the location in the media are usually received with a call from the Church's lawyers. They claim to represent Michele and have said that she's committed to full-time Church activities.

Update

Because of the failures of these investigation, the only information that we have comes via former Scientology members Scientology who have spoken with the media. A lot of these stories indicate that Michele is in the Church's compound, which is a complex devoted to "Spiritual technology." It is located in California Access to people who aren't members of the Church is not allowed. An ex-financial officer of the Church's head David Miscavige has stated that David gave his wife an item of clothing as well as a pair of gloves for Christmas the year prior. The report does not specify if Michele received the presents. Perhaps the most troubling of all are the speculations from members that suggest Michele could have been taken to the location called "The The Hole" an California facility run through Scientology.

Church of Scientology about which very little is known, besides reports of punishment and forced work. Because of the power of the Church as well as its secretive ways that they conceal their secrets from the public the truthful details of Michele's disappearance will never to be revealed in the light of day. As more critical investigations of Scientology being reported on the news, Michele might provide the solution to uncovering the secrets that lie within one of the most bizarre organizations.

The girl of a small age who was famous for disappearing from her parents' custody
Who: Madeleine McCann
When: 3 May 2007.
Where: Praia da Luz, Portugal
Context
If there's any incident that better illustrates the ways in which missing people can provoke both public support and criticism and even public criticism, that of the missing Madeleine McCann is it. The case is still extensively discussed in the British media following an

international hunt this case is among the world's most well-known and also one of the most confusing. Unsolved to date, the manner the various people involved - from the parents of Madeleine as well as the Portuguese police were treated highlights the varying opinions and feelings that could be present, as well as the bizarre fascination that the media can have with the disappearance of a child.

At the time of her disappearance, Madeleine was just three years old. With no background that she could claim, a lot of the background is from the life of her parents, Kate as well as Gerald. Both McCanns were committed Roman Catholics and accredited physicians. They had started dating in 1993 and got married five years after. Madeleine was their first child who was born in. The couple also had a set twins a few years after. The year 2007 was the time they went on an extended family trip to Portugal.

That day

When Kate and Gerald were able to see Madeleine she was asleep. They decided to take her to an evening meal with a selected group of friends. They left their daughter sleeping in their hotel room. The restaurant they picked was just a few hundred yards from the hotel. When Kate was taking a break from dinner to check in on her kids, Madeleine was gone.

The first thing to happen was that the police were notified. A huge search that involved many hotel guests and hotel staff was conducted to locate the missing child of three years. The border police were informed and Spanish airports and police were put on alert. With the number of volunteers increasing by the hour The hunt of Madeleine McCann turned up nothing.

The investigation

The following day, Madeleine's parents released a statement detailing their despair and grief. Police in the area identified an individual they wanted to speak to, and reiterated it was their opinion that girl was alive and living in the United States. As police searched, McCann's released a second statement calling for information regarding Madeleine.

The first suspect identified to be identified was Robert Murat, who had been born in Britain. The police named him as an official suspect investigators. The police conducted a search of the home where his mother was living close to 150 yards from the house where the McCanns were in. This was not a success.

The next step was to release a sketch of a man who'd been observed in the area on that night with either the child or an object that could be thought to be an infant. In addition, Kate McCann began to be interrogated by police in the area. In the following months, police acknowledged that crucial forensic evidence were lost during the course of the investigation, in the days following Madeleine was taken away due to inadequate protection of the scene of the crime.

There were no concrete leads however, investigators from the British police flies over various sniffer dogs, designed to locate tiny blood traces as well as the close proximity of dead bodies. They were trained to sniff out the locations where the McCanns have stayed as well as cars connected to the investigation as well as the rental vehicle the family was using.

100 days after Madeleine disappeared, investigators eventually conceded that the girl may be dead. They also said that the parents of Madeleine weren't being considered suspects, but the media began to make fun of the McCann's tale. After these accusations that the McCann family filed the libel suit against an Portuguese newspaper, which had published a report on suspicions by police of murder. Madeleine.

The next calendar month Kate McCann was again detained by the local police and was this time held during 11 hours. The lawyer of the victim was present during the interrogation. The next day, local police made the two "persons worth mentioning" in the investigation. A representative of the McCann family says that detectives found tiny amounts of Madeleine's blood inside the vehicle that the family hired. The McCann family returned back to Britain the following day. The police in the area dismissed possibility that the blood could be a perfect match to the blood of Madeleine's.

Over the course of the next few weeks, detectives from Portugal began to assert that there was not enough evidence to justify the questioning of parents. Additionally the head detective in the case was dismissed from his post following numerous public complaints against his British colleagues. In his place the deputy national director for Portugal's police force was chosen to lead the investigation into the disappearance.

Another request to find out more information was made by the parents of Madeleine. Gerald recording a video of his suspicions that there was a "predator" had followed and watched his family during the days leading towards his daughter's disappearance. After a few months after the disappearance, the McCann family was able to publish sketches of a person they believe is linked to the investigation, created by analyzing the description of the "creepy" person who was mentioned in the Christmas report. The family was then able to accept more than 500,000 pounds in damages for libel from British media outlets that been able to link them to the incident.

To try to make an effort to make local police flew out to Britain to observe firsthand the British police questioning those who were at dining room with McCanns at the time of the questions. The group was dubbed by the name of Tapas Seven. In the following days they were Portuguese authorities were forced deny they released Kate and Gerald's initial statements to the media. This included the idea that Madeleine could have been upset at the time of the disappearance, and that after an argument her mother may not have contacted her in tears.

When the investigation was about to reach one year The family issued an emotional statement in which they asked the public to keep their prayers open for Madeleine as the family celebrated the tragic anniversary. The Portuguese police chief who was on the case was accused of being insensitive to the manner in which he dealt with the case, and was forced to resign. In the wake of this, local police were required to submit what they call the "final report" regarding the incident that was later scrutinized. The McCanns were deemed not to be noteworthy in the matter in the eyes of Portuguese authorities, and so did Robert Murat, who accepted the settlement of a substantial amount in a libel matter.

An ex-lead investigator in the case has published an autobiography detailing his experiences and theories regarding missing Madeleine on July 1st, less than one year after she disappeared. He said that the girl was killed in the McCann's home for holidays. The McCann family says they'll sue him for the allegations.

In November of that year, British authorities released a video that showed photos of what Madeleine could look like just two years to the day since her went missing. The video is available in seven different languages, but yields nothing new information. In the meantime, Kate and Gerald release an autobiography detailing their experience of the investigation into their daughter's disappearance.

With only a few new details as of now, the possibility was fading of ever being able to find Madeleine alive or not. A 2000-page report was made public which contained numerous possible sightings of a small girl, but none was able to lead to any kind of conclusion. The third anniversary of the disappearance was near, her father confessed to being extremely frustrated by the inability to make progress provided by police, which suggested that they hadn't been in search of his daughter for a lengthy period of time. When the case began to fade away from attention by the press, but it was being re-read by certain British and Portuguese publications.

Update

While this case was discussed numerous times when the investigation was brought to a standstill, no changes have been seen. The McCann family has contacted the British prime minister to initiate an investigation into the matter. They've published an account of their experience to raise funds to help their daughter's fund. The family has been involved in the infamous Leveson cellphone hacking case and since then there are new and up-to-date photos that show how Madeleine could look if caught today.

2013 was the year that British investigators who were investigating the case reported that they'd discovered a variety of new people they wanted to talk to. They published e-fit profiles (electronic face identification) of these individuals and broadcast the profiles in UK television. Further investigations have suggested that phone records may be the key to solving the case, however no new methods are able to solve the mystery. In spite of this, British police are still conducting investigations, even though it's unclear what amount of manpower is involved in the case. At present, we don't know what transpired to Madeleine or in what way her parents, police, certain people or others were involved in the investigation. There are no concrete leads and no concrete theories, Madeleine McCann will remain in the dark for the time being.

CHAPTER 4: WHAT IS THE CAUSE? ALIENS HAVE A HAND IN THIS PECULIAR DISAPPEARING INSTANCE?

Who is: Frederick Valentich

Date: 21st October 1978

Location: Bass Strait, Australia

Context

People who are missing aren't limited only to United States. As mentioned in the first two chapters 8 million people every year are missing. The way in which different countries handle these challenges can help us understand the differences in culture which exist across the globe. Since there aren't all countries with America's resources , or the type of terrain that is known, finding individuals in countries like Australia is a challenge. For instance, the disappearance of Frederick Valentich is one such case of someone disappearing in Australia. Frederick Valentich was just 20-years old when he disappeared in the Australia's Bass Strait. He was on the road for a hundred miles journey, a training flight to teach him the basics of how to fly his Cessna lightweight aircraft. On the 21st of October 1978, he'd find the limits of his aircraft's capabilities.

The story isn't so simple as just disappearing of a man. Another aspect is added by Valentich's openly confessed love for flying saucers. In the event of his last transmission, it's that fascination that lingers on the transmission.

That day

On the day he vanished, Frederick Valentich was flying across the Bass Straight. At 6 minutes past 7 hours, he hopped on his radio and made contact with the flight control station at Melbourne. He was looking to inform them of the unidentified object flying overhead an unknown plane that began to follow the man. It was a massive vehicle with four lights that flashed on its side. Valentich called these lights lighting fixtures as landing lights. While unable to indicate the kind of aircraft that was in flight control, it crossed just three hundred meters over him at an incredible speed. Valentich continued to relay his location in the presence of the radio operators, implying that the driver of another aircraft was playing with him, advancing toward him at an extremely fast speed, and then getting his plane into orbit. From this, Valentich could see the machine's shiny surface and its green glow. At this moment, he started to talk about the engine. The radio operator demanded Valentich to find the other flier, to which he responded that it wasn't an aircraft. At the end of this transmission, the voice faded out, and the radio operator was only able to hear what he described as "metallic scraping sounds." Then all contact with Valentich disappeared.

The investigation

The investigation was conducted by the Australian Department of Transport (DOT). In the course of their investigations they were unable identify the exact cause that caused Valentich's plane to break up, but they believed that the result were fatal. There was no wreckage was discovered or reported, and nobody was able to provide the crash site of Valentich's flight. The site was not discovered until five years later, after the incident after the flap of the cowl of an engine was discovered on the shores of Flinders Island. It was determined that it was identical to the flap that was found in Valentich's Cessna 182, lying within the number of serial numbers which matched his aircraft. However, they couldn't determine for sure if it exactly was the cowl flap. This leaves conclusive evidence of the lighter side.

Update

Because of the circumstances surrounding that disappearance Frederick Valentich, the event that caused his disappearance caused a lot of attention from across his Australian border. A peculiarity that was discovered was that the fuel used on his flight was supposed to be able to transport him for over eight hundred miles. However, there's no trace of his flight in any location in the radar of his assumed course, suggesting that he could be wildly off the track. There's even a report from the police of Melbourne which suggests that a small aircraft made an unconfirmed landing just a few miles from Valentich's proposed route approximately at the exact same moment. However, nothing has been verified.

A theory is that Valentich could have been flying upside-down after becoming disoriented while flying. This could explain the sight that he believed he saw and the green lights as the reflection of his aircraft on the sea, and the bizarre motions being his own interaction in his reflection. The radio operator could then be able to hear his crash into the ocean. Another possibility is the possibility of suicide although no reason is known the reason Valentich would want to commit suicide.

Some of the most bizarre theories have been that were put forth by those who are who are the most fascinated (as Valentich himself was) in the UFO aspect of the tale. The notion that aliens could have abducted or attacked him has been reportedly put forth but they aren't considered to be popular with many. An extraterrestrial group located in Phoenix, Arizona have claimed that they have matched photos taken by an individual who was near to the incident, pictures which show the type of swiftly moving, green-lit object that Valentich says he has witnessed. As with all the most bizarre theories the evidence for this one is being searched for. If you're looking to discover an answer to the question, the account of Frederick Valentich provides nothing in terms of satisfactory answers. A UFO enthusiast to die in such circumstances as this might be a bit odd but his name will soon add to the countless thousands of people who disappear every year.

A mysterious disappearance district attorney

The person: Ray Gricar

Date: April 15th, 2005

Location: Lewisburg, Pennsylvania

Context: Although certain cases we've looked at have been a bit spooky and a possibility that you can solve a missing persons case is not without sparking the interest of the public. The situation of Ray Gricar, the mysterious circumstances that led to his death suggested that even the tiniest hint that the mystery could be solved led to an online campaign.

Before his disappearance Ray Gricar would not have been able to draw the attention of. In 1945, the man went on to become an attorney, and eventually served as the District Attorney of Centre County, Pennsylvania. The position was held until the day that he vanished. He was a successful candidate for reelection at least four times during his time in office, showing that he was popular in his post. However it took an additional six years for them to pronounce him dead as a result of the absence of evidence of his disappearance.

That day

The date was April 15th in 2005. The time was just 11 am in the early morning. Gricar had made a phone call to his girlfriend whom he shared a house. He explained that he would be driving and that the trip was going to take it across the Brush Valley region. However, despite his promises, he never got at home. He was reported missing the next night.

The investigation

The next day, investigators discovered a car that resembled Ray's that was an Red Mini Cooper - in the parking lot of an Lewisburg antiques shop. Inside was Gricar's cell phone (work issued) and his other belongings weren't discovered, such as a computer, a wallet, as well as his keys. In addition the police found no indications that any foul play was involved. The Ray's family members that the location of the car was like the location of his brother's car close to the location in which Roy killed himself a couple of years ago. Following the discovery of Ray's vehicle investigators began looking at the river that was nearby and the banks around it, but were unable to find any trace of Gricar. After finding nothing tangible or physical, the authorities in the area requested that the FBI investigate the bank account of the person who disappeared as well as credit card and cell phone in order to find out the reason for death of the district prosecutor. They found nothing.

Update

But, the story doesn't end there. In July of 2005 the laptop that was used to work for Gricar was found by a fisherman in the river nearby. It was found under the bridge and was given to authorities who identified that it was belonging to Ray Gricar. One of the first things they noticed in analyzing this device was that it had no drive. The hard drive was discovered 2 months later, 100 yards away from the river's shores. river. Even though the hard drive was discovered however, it was badly damaged to be able to retrieve any data or to conduct any meaningful analysis. It appeared that this finding did not offer any further information about the disappearance of Gricar.

A few years later, the police discovered that in the period before he went missing gone missing, someone utilized Ray's desktop computer at the house that he shared with his girlfriend. The user had utilized the computer to conduct search seeking more details on how to damage or destroy the hard drive on a computer. In addition they searched for additional information on the ways to damage the laptop by with water. However, nothing else came from this info.

The case was made the subject of two documentaries broadcast on TV. They have helped make the public aware of the case and also to inform the public about the mysterious circumstances that led to Ray Gricar vanished. It wasn't until 2011 , that the daughter of Ray,

Lara was able to ask an appeals court for the declaration of Ray officially dead.

A day later one day later, a man was arrested in Utah who refused to reveal his true identity. He was charged with a misdemeanor The John Doe had an equivalence to many of the physical traits of Gricar that included similar weight, height as well as a similar lip shape and even the same position of facial wrinkles. As time passed, many online began to speculate John Doe could be the identical Ray Gricar. Due to the amount of attention this case was getting local police sent copies of Gricar's fingerprints the Utah colleagues. After a brief spurt of curiosity, the police in Utah were able to confirm that the fingerprints didn't coincide. It was not Ray Gricar. Despite the awe-inspiring amount of attention that the case received recently the detectives had not come any further away from locating the missing person.

One of the world's pioneering filmmakers disappears before reaping the benefits of his creation

Who: Louis Le Prince
Date: 16 September 1890
Location: Dijon, France

Context

Like disappearances that can happen throughout America and across the world It can be very difficult to remember how they are dealt with by different people in various cultures. The instance that occurred with Louis Le Prince demonstrates how such a situation could have been handled in the 19th century France. To provide a perspective on the time between then and the present, Le Prince is one of the people who are credited for helping to create cinema as we see it in the present. His motion pictures taken with single lens cameras were the precursor to the present-day video camera. Due to this his work, he is referred to as the cinematographer's father by a few.

The majority of Le Prince's research and development was carried out in Leeds, the English town of Leeds. Le Prince travelled throughout Europe and America to refine his ideas, however, it was in October 1888 when Le Prince first showed his motion pictures in sequences. These were created with an camera with only just one lens, and one roll film made of paper. The images were of bridges in Leeds and were released a few times before more famous and well-known camera creators made their debut on the stage.

While he had planned on showing off his inventions in America however, it never came to realization. After his disappearance, his ideas and work would vanish and Thomas Edison taking the credit for the many inventions. The wife of Le Prince and his son were determined to preserve Louis's legacy and went to the courts to fight Edison who claimed that he was the first, most important and the sole filmmaker's inventor. The significance of this legal fight was the fact that it determined who would receive the royalties from the invention. The court would ultimately rule against Edison following Louis's son's request that he was denied permission to show two cameras before the court and to show the world his father had invented the camera prior to his competitor. This was the setting that Le Prince mysteriously vanished, his legacy that led to the billion-dollar industries we see to this day in the field of film.

That day

At the time of his death in 1880 Louis began to prepare for a return to England in the hopes of obtaining patents on the camera technology that was his creation. The journey across America in United States that September had been planned to increase publicity for the camera, but Louis was already missing his family and friends. When he arrived in France at the time of departure, he set off from Bourges at the time of 13th of September, taking a train to Dijon to visit his brother. The plan was to take an additional train the following day, to bring him straight to Paris. As the train arrived at the station Le Prince was nowhere to be seen. Le Prince could never be ever seen again. In the train's search and the train, there was not a trace of a body nor any baggage he could bring with him. Investigators even scanned the tracks of the railway between Paris as well as Dijon but came up empty. He was never noticed by anyone as his brother left on the platform. Nothing unusual or odd behaviors were observed on the train, and none of the passengers remember having seen him.

The investigation

The investigation was managed by various organizations, including the French police and British Scotland Yard. Additionally his family members chose to conduct an investigation independently. Although nobody could offer a definitive explanation, there were four theories that have been proposed through the use of evidence collected by different groups.

The most popular theory refers to suicide. Cinema journalist Georges Potonniee recalls being told by one of Louis's family members that the inventor wanted to commit suicide should he discover that his company was soon to become insolvent. The death was planned to allow for the deportation of the body as well as the baggage that would be on the train. In spite of the suggestions from family members, the historian says that the business of Le Prince continued to make profitable profits at the time, which means Le Prince was still far from the end of his savings which could lead to suicide attempts.

Another theory, however, is far more dangerous. It puts Edison in the middle of an assassination plot to kill Le Prince, ensuring that the patents for the moving image technology would be under Edison's possession. At the time Louis went missing, Louis was on the close to patenting his famous projection techniques in Britain and later in America. The theory is believed to be appealing to Louis's wife even though there is a dearth of evidence in support of this. The court case that involved Le Prince's son clearly demonstrates the importance of the patents and the degree to that Edison was willing to fight for intellectual rights to the technology. The son in the court case passed away himself in mysterious circumstances, found dead while shoot ducks within New York. New York area.

Perhaps even more sinister is the idea that Le Prince's family could be involved in his demise. A film scholar, Jacques Deslandes, suggested in the sixties that Le Prince was willing to disappear, partly because of financial motives and also due to rumors that began to circulate about his sexuality. The time of homosexuality was still considered a crime and some historians suggest it was because Le Prince extracted himself willingly from the situation in order to protect his family's image. There's a lot little evidence to support this idea it is a rare case that people consider it worthy of weight.

There is also a claim it was Le Prince was the victim of murder, murdered by his brother, who watched him leave Dijon. If Le Prince wanted to disappear by himself He could have gone missing at any time. But, Jean Mitry casts doubts about the role played by Louis's brother in her disappearance, and the fact that he did not actually leave out of the railway station at Dijon as we've been taught to believe. Again the absence of evidence creates a serious problem in determining the truth of the theories.

Update: Despite the numerous speculations, Louis Le Prince was declared dead in 1897. In the absence of his body, Thomas Edison was able to patent the cinematography method and establish the film industry we have today. We won't know for sure what transpired to Louis but a fascinating footnote was found in 2003, as investigators in Paris began to look through the police archives in search of a single image dating back to 1890. The person in the photograph was drowned, and he had an eerie resemblance to Louis Le Prince. It is unclear if it was Louis Le Prince. we won't know for sure.

CHAPTER 5: THE STORY OF AN ACTRESS WHO GAINED FAME WHEN SHE WENT MISSING

Whois: Jean Spangler

Date: 7 October 1949

The location: Los Angeles, California

Context

One of the main draws to Hollywood is the romanticized, beautiful version that is in the minds of those who are attracted with the town. This was especially true during the 1940s, this West Coast film-making capital being the first stop for those who were even remotely interested in the field of entertainment. The chance to go large was at hand and a lot of people attempted. But , in the end, it did not go as planned. The case of Jean Spangler was that her shift to Hollywood was a mistake that would make her famous for completely different reasons.

The girl was raised in rainierand more colder climate of Seattle and grew into a dancer with some talent. She made the choice to relocate to California where she resided alongside her parents Florence as well as Edward and Sophie as well as her brother and wife. They lived in a complex located in Park La Brea in the city of Los Angeles. The year 1942 was when she was married to Dexter Benner, a man who was interested in manufacturing. The couple eventually split in 1942, and they sent Jean home to her compound. They awarded her parental rights to their little girl Christine (who was just five years old).

On the same day

in 1949 Jean quit the home on October 7 , 5 hours. Christine was left behind with Sophie because Jean stated that she was going to meet Dexter in order to talk about issue of late payments of child support due. Then she was off to a film location on which she was taking part in a shoot at night. The last person to meet Jean Spangler was one of the employees the local shop near the family home. He commented that Jean seemed to be standing waiting for the arrival of an additional person. The mother of the girl, Florence wasn't at the house at the time , so it fell to Sophie to notify Jean as missing that she reported the next day.

The investigation

The investigation started when Jean was found missing. The first thing to be checked was the film location at which Jean stated she would be staying the night. As police looked into this possibility, the course of inquiry ended in a deadlock. After contacting the studios that could have offered to work with her however, none of them seemed to be carrying out any type of work that evening. There was nowhere Jean might have been able to visit to do work on the set.

The next suspect would be Dexter the former husband of Jean. The man was asked about her travels, Sophie telling authorities that the absence of child support was the cause of Jean's trip. Dexter however, maintained that he hadn't seen Jean for several weeks. Since he had remarried, his new wife was in a position to give him an excuse for the period which the police were looking for.

After a few days the purse of Jean was found in the vicinity of one of the entryways into the city of Los the city's Griffith Park. There was evidence of damage and the straps were broken as if they was taken by her hand. The police enlisted sixty officers and 100 volunteers to search the park in search of additional clues. They did not find anything. The money that was stored in the purse was taken away, but Sophie claimed that Jean was not carrying any money when she was leaving the house. The police dismissed the possibility of robbery as a motive to the disappearance. There was a note inside the purse, but it was an incomplete letter addressed to a person named Kirk. The note advised Kirk that she wouldn't be able to stay in the waiting room long and was scheduled to visit the Doctor Scott that even. The letter concluded with a statement that it was the "best method" to deal with the situation when Jean's mother was gone. The letter concluded with a comma to indicate there was some more to follow.

After a thorough search, the police did not locate any person who would match the description of the names Dr. Scott or Kirk. Jean's relatives and acquaintances could inform the police that they could not find anyone who resembled those names that she could have come across. When Florence returned home, she made mention that a person going by his name as Kirk was able to collect Jean several times from the home of her family. In those instances the man remained in the vehicle and not made any introductions. Any doctor who had the surname Scott was investigated however, no one could give details about patients who were under Jean's name.

The second lead was an earlier job Jean had finished, which was filming a small part in the film Young Man, which starred the famous actor Kirk Douglas. Douglas was on vacation, way out from Palm Springs. When he was informed of Jean's disappearance, he made an email to officers to let them know of his location as well as his alibi. He also wanted to state that he could not and could not have been an individual who was the Kirk of the note. After being questioned by police, he admitted that he knew of Jean's involvement as an extra, but was unaware of the identity of Jean.

It was discovered that Jean was pregnant for three months. She thought about being induced to have an abortion a number of her acquaintances. The procedure was not legal in the time, and was likely to cause a lot of anxiety. The people who lived within the same circles of social interaction as Jean informed police that there was an individual referred to by the name of "doc" who was able to perform the procedure. But, the police were unable to locate the man, or even figure out if there was a man in the first instance.

It was discovered that Jean was observed having a conversation with a man named Davy Ogul, who had relationships with a variety of prominent criminals. Ogul disappeared two days prior to Jean. The police began looking at possible evidence that Jean and Ogul were deliberately hiding in order to avoid the increasing legal issues that Ogul was at the in the middle of. In 1950, a clerk at an Texan hotel claimed that he'd seen two persons with similar names like these two, however their names didn't appear to be connected to the register or within the immediate vicinity.

Update

The searching for Jean Spangler went on for a long time. After her disappearance, Jean became far more popular than she had been in her film roles. Then, there was a one thousand dollars reward offered for information that could result in her being found. The calls came from across the country, yet nobody was able to locate Jean down. As of today police from the Los Angeles Police Department have opened the case indefinitely. Jean Spangler is still listed as missing.

A case of disappearing twins

Who are: Katherine as well as Sheila Lyon

Date when: March 25, 1975

The location: Wheaton, Maryland

Context

Although the case of a missing person's disappearance can draw the attention of the public however, it could just as easily be swept under the rug by a more significant story. The case of Lyon sisters, an incident which would normally be featured on the front pages of all newspapers was pushed off the radar when it was announced there was a possibility that it was likely that United States would be pulling out of its conflict with Vietnam. But the story is fascinating in its own way.

They Lyon sisters were daughter of John Lyon and his wife Mary. They had a younger sibling and a brother named John who later went to join the police department. Their dad, John, was somewhat famous in the local community and was well-known for hosting a radio show on station WMAL which was operated by ABC television. John was later employed as counsellor for victims and helped others overcome the tragic events. This is the place where Katherine as well as Sheila Lyon were born and the house that they left.

On the same day

On the day they vanished The two sisters were just half a mile from their house after having travelled through the Wheaton Plaza mall. They were out on the 25th of March 1975 to view the exhibitions that were exhibited to celebrate

Easter. While away of school the couple were planning to enjoy the spring break exploring an area Orange Bowl for lunch. They left home at noon, and received the strict instruction of their mom that they return to their home by 4 hours. When they did not return home until late in the night, parents alerted police, who started an exhaustive search of the location. Even though the timeframe was verified by their parents but the police did not believe in its reliability to reveal the information to the public.

There were reports from witnesses. In the afternoon, a kid from the nearby neighborhood reported having seen one or perhaps both girls in a group just outside of their restaurant that was at the Orange Bowl. The same child informed officers that he remembered seeing them talk to a male whom he was unable to be able to identify. A few hours later the child's brother John remembers seeing them in the same restaurant eating an evening meal. A half hour later an individual girl's acquaintances was able to recall seeing the Lyon sisters heading west along the street that runs near to the mall, a road that would have brought them back straight to their home. It was the time at which they left that police were confirmed to be absolutely the girls. Since they were not able to get at home, the police started their investigation.

The investigation

The man that was reported to be speaking to girls outside the Orange Bowl quickly became a central point of inquiry. He was reported to have been about six feet tall, and possibly older than 50 or even 60. And the man was wearing the brown color of his suit. He carried a briefcase that contained a recording tool, that a lot of children in the mall were reported to use recording their voices on tape and replaying it. Based on the description of the witness that led to the investigation's principal suspect and they compiled two sketches that show the man's appearance.

Next, the next task was follow for reports from people who claimed they recognized the man in sketches. There are reports linking the man not identified with Marlow Heights mall and the Iverson Mall. Marlow Heights mall and the Iverson mall, both located in the area.

According to these reports, the man was walking up to girls of a young age, and asking girls to talk into the microphone in order they could record their voices. It was as if they were trying to make an answering machine and gave children a written paper to write their message on. There was no public announcement by the investigators that linked these reports to the girls who disappeared the evidence began to fade away.

For those with hopes to find girls group of volunteers started to search the parking lot as well as the river bed within the local region. The search continued for these next days as the media got more more involved. In the end, National Guard was even recruited to assist in the search to find the lost Lyon sisters and the search was extended into The Montgomery County forest. The remains or trace of Katherine as well as Sheila Lyon was ever found.

Update

When the attention of the media increased to a high level the shocking announcement of the United States' withdrawal from Vietnam became the focus of the media. The focus shifted, and might have reduced the likelihood of locating the suspect or locating the girls. In spite of this it is true that there have been a number of suspects connected to the case throughout the years.

One of the first victims was Fred Coffey, who was sentenced to prison for life in 1987 following his beating and strangled the little girl from North Carolina. The authorities discovered that Coffey was present in the region on the day of the incident and had been conducted an interview for a job in nearby Silver Spring, Maryland. Authorities have not been able to connect Coffey to the investigation however. There are no charges related to the Lyon sisters have been brought against him.

Another possible suspect is an individual by the name or Raymond Mileski, who lived in the area around 1975. His residence in Suitland is close to the spot within Prince George's County where a man was recording sounds of kids. Mileski was found guilty of murdering his wife and son, and also assaulting another son in 1977. The information provided by people in the prison as well as clues from Mileski himself, suggest that he was aware of some details about the disappearances from the girl. He was willing to provide his information in exchange for lenient conditions while in prison. The police who later conducted a search of his house and discovered nothing or evidence of crime, and Mileski died in the year 2004.

We will never know the fate of these Lyon sisters. Their names are now on the list of thousands of others whose real story is never revealed. The thing that is most fascinating however is the chance of their finding had the media been able concentrate on the story in greater depth. As the country changed direction on the matter, the investigation was likely affected in some way by the close in the Vietnam War.

Two generations leave the same house at one night...

Whoare they? The Springfield Three

Date: 7 June 1992

The location: Springfield, Missouri

Context

Many of the cases we've covered have focused on people who disappeared or even a pair who vanished, seldom does it happen that three persons suffer the same circumstances. If one person is one of the victims in an accident, catastrophe that affects more than one person is much less likely, particularly when there are three. This leads to foul play in the equation and the possibility of criminal charges becoming more complicated when more people get involved. One example of this happens however, is the case of"the" Springfield Three.

The story starts with Sherrill Levitt, who was 47, at the time the incident occurred. She was petite taller than five feet and weighing in at just 110lbs. Her blonde hair was cut in a short bob. Her eyes were brown. She worked as a hairdresser in the town nearby and was a mother-in-law for her young daughter Suzanne Streeter. The two were described as extremely close with the daughter being slightly larger and lighter. For Suzanne the latter, she was spotted with an identifiable scar on her left forearm and a small mole that was left on her lip. The third suspect was a friend of Suzanne's who was a girl named Stacy McCall, who was aged 18 and was similar in appearance to the girl she was with.

That day

The day before the incident was particularly important in the lives of Stacy and Suzanne. Stacy and Suzanne since they both graduated from high school. It was the last time their peers would get to hear from them. The last time she spoke to them was via an email shortly after midnight that night in which she talked to a colleague about the color scheme of an old cabinet. The girls last seen around 2:00 in the morning, after leaving the graduation celebration that was held at the home of a friend. They had been planning to stay the night at the house of a friend, however, this home became too overcrowded. They decided to stay time at Suzanne's residence which was in which Sherrill was believed to be asleep sleeping. We can speculate that they were there, since their cars, jewelry and other possessions were found on the house.

Thirteen hours later, after having no contact about their daughter, and also not being able to locate her Stacey's parents put in an emergency call to police in the area. Others from the family and friends were in contact, with no knowledge of the location for any women. They were the worried family members and friends who police later concluded had that they had contaminated the scene of incident by visiting Sherrill and Suzanne's residence in search of their acquaintances. The home was not contaminated, and there were no indications or signs of a fight within, as was observed by the police officers who arrived at the scene. One sign was a light that was broken above the patio, that was removed and cleaned by the visitors. Sherrill's bed was used however all the property like purses, keys money, cars, and keys were still on the property. Even the dog from the family was at home. The woman had disappeared.

The investigation

One of the investigation's principal leads in the investigation was the testimony to Robert Cox, a man who was previously found guilty of robbery and kidnapping. As a suspect in the case of a murder in Florida He told authorities that he knew that the three women were victims of a crime and were put to rest in a location where they were never to be found. In the following days, Cox informed officers that his evening was spent with his partner in the area the night when the three women were missing. Then Cox denied the claim, claiming it was the house of his parents and they were able to confirm his claim. The police reported that they were unsure about what to do with Cox's confession and wondered if the man was just looking for attention. Today, Cox insists that he will provide more information after the passing of his mother.

Update

In the absence of leads and no evidence, the inquiry into the disappearance of three women the night of the murder remains unsolved. In spite of the more than 5,000 tips shared by the general public. In 1997 the unveiling of a bench dedicated to the missing women who were missing from the Phelps Grove Park in Springfield. The case gained some degree of fame after being mentioned on several of America's most well-known crime shows such as "America's most wanted." But, despite this however, the case hasn't been resolved, and detectives have not been enthusiastic about solving the case. It is either Cox will divulge his information regarding the bodies at a date he believes is appropriate or the location of Sherrill, Suzanne, and Stacey will not be revealed.

CHAPTER 6: A TERRIFYING EXPERIENCE OF A WOMAN WHO WAS BELIEVED TO BE GONE

The person: Jaycee Lee Dugard
Date: 10 June 1991
The location: Lake Tahoe, California

Context

In a lot of the cases we have looked at to date, the individual's disappearance remains unsolved. In other words, the manner in the manner in which they disappeared has not been clear, and there are many witnesses to the incident. In certain instances there have been instances in where witnesses have witnessed the abduction of a person and then been able to remain missing. One of these cases is of Jaycee Lee Dugard.

Jaycee along with her entire family relocated into a rural region near Lake Tahoe in September of 1990, hoping that it would be the security they needed from their previous residence within Orange County. Jaycee was in the fifth grade at the time she disappeared. She was concerned about a forthcoming field trip, and said she was shy and hard to conquer. She had a strong bond with her mother Terry Probyn, as did their younger brother. The family was separated by her father's biological father, however, her mother had remarried. Her husband was known as Carl Probyn. Jacyee was not close with him.

That day

It was June 10 1991. This was the year that followed the relocation. Terry (Jacyee's mom) was getting ready for her new job in a printing house. She was on her way to work in the early hours of that day. Jaycee was planning to wear her most favored pink dress and was making the climb to the top of the hill from her residence to take the bus to school. She was walking along the crowd when, at the midpoint of the hill she came to a stop by a passing vehicle. As she thought that the man could be seeking directions, she stopped to help him. Phillip Garrido was sat at the wheel. He opened the window to knock Jaycee unconscious with stun guns. He then dragged her into the vehicle where Nancy Garrido, Phillip's wife was able to grab the girl. They kidnapped her and took her to the house of the Garrido's which is located just two hours from Antioch. All Jaycee could offer during this time was to assure the kidnappers her parents wouldn't be able to pay an amount of ransom.

The main person who was a witness of the kidnapping is Carl Probyn, Jaycee's stepfather who observed a grey sedan and two individuals make a one sharp right at the stop for buses. While pulling close to Jaycee and her stepfather, he witnessed them drag her inside the vehicle. He attempted to chase them with a bicycle but was not able to get them out of the vehicle. In addition to Probyn there were other members of Jaycee's school remember having seen something. Of the suspects initially, Probyn and Jaycee's biological father were among those who were the most often asked questions.

When she arrived at the home of Garrido, Jaycee had had her clothing taken away. The only thing she kept was a tiny butterfly-shaped ring she concealed. She was brought in blankets from the vehicle , and then taken to the property, along the gardenand then into the

118

space where the Garridos had numerous storage and sheds. One of them was specifically sealed off from sound. This is where Philip Garrido raped and handcuffed his victim left her unclothed in her shed that was locked behind him. He then left with the message that the dog was snooping in the open and under strict orders to attack if she tried to get away.

The investigation

It was only a couple of hours for the media to take to the report that was told about Jaycee Dugard. Local and national news organizations visited the region to the south from Lake Tahoe, driving the national coverage of the kidnapping. Soon after, the volunteers began searching for any source they could imagine covering the local community and using all resources. A plethora of fliers and posters are printed out and handed out. Jaycee's name became common information. The leaflets were distributed and distributed across the country in hopes that someone would recognize the girl. The town decided to wrap its own town with pink ribbons representing Jaycee's favourite color as the show of support and solidarity with her family.

The mother of Jaycee's established the group called Jaycee's Hope that was used to coordinate the search and fundraising in the region. It involved buttons, clothing and even an audio cassette to increase awareness about the disappearance of the girl. Authorities at the federal level offered help and assistance. The reward was announced with the reward's details included on the poster. The case was featured in one of America's most popular crime TV shows, "America's Most Wanted." But the efforts failed.

The next April the following April, a phone call was made to the sheriff's office in the area informing them that a girl was seen looking in awe at one of the posters that were missing before being taken to the back of the yellow van. The van had disappeared when police were able to arrive on the site. Nobody had obtained information about the plate. The caller did not identify themselvesand police could not connect any of the evidence to locate the woman.

Update

The trail was icy. In this period, Jaycee - missing to the world, remained alive. She was kept in Garrido's shed, sexually assaulted by her captor and impregnated. In this period she claims she was not allowed to leave the house until just before she gave birth to her baby that occurred in 1994. Authorities had no idea to believe that Garrido might have been involved in the incident, despite his previous involvement in a kidnapping and sexual assault in 1976 in a similar location to the one in which Jaycee was kidnapped.

In 2002, nearly 10 years later, firemen arrived at the site of a shoulder injury that occurred in the Garrido's house where a minor was reported as being injured in the pool. The incident was not reported to Garrido's parole officers, even though there was no previous evidence of a juvenile or child in the home.

Four years later, in 2004, police received a call from 911 to inform children who lived at Garrido's house in a group of tents located in the backyard. They also were told the Garrido is "psychotic" and was addicted to sexual activity.

A sheriff came to the home to inquire and talk with Garrido in front of the house. They spoke for 30 minutes. The sheriff left after notifying Garrido of the possibility of violation if people were camping on his property.

As of 2009 Garrido traveled to San Francisco offices of the FBI and wrote an essay that outlined his views regarding sexuality and religion. This essay of four pages explained the ways he discovered solutions for sexual addiction and provided tips on how to reverse it in other people. Then, he attended the University of California with his two daughters (Jaycee's daughters) and sought permission to host an event. He was asked to schedule an appointment. By leaving his address and contact details an initial background check revealed that he was a sexual offender. After he returned the following day, the officer from the local area took note of the unattractive girls and left the details of the encounter in the voicemails at the parole offices.

The message was sent to Garrido's parole officers who went to go to his home the next day. Garrido was arrested and the house was went through a search. This only found Garrido's wife Nancy and his aging mother. Garrido was then brought back in the office of parole to be questioned. Even though he had committed violations to his parole due to the trip with two girls - whom Garrido claimed were daughters of a family member - the officers ignored the issue and requested Garrido to appear before them on the next day. Garrido arrived at the office with his entire family, including Jacyee who is known as Allissa as well as the two girls. The family was separated, and were asked to provide the identification of one another. After more than 15 years in captivity Jaycee continued to believe in the illusions that was created by the captor. She claimed that Garrido was an "great individual." The comments were accepted by the children. The police demanded more details, which forced Jaycee to defend herself. Jaycee spewed another story that the police investigated. As pressure mounted, Garrido confessed to kidnapping and robbing the girl, at the she admitted to the crime. Jaycee acknowledged her true identity. Garrido was detained. Jaycee was returned to her mother, who had been working for years to raise funds to locate her daughter who was missing.

If this book had been written a couple of years earlier, the trial of Jaycee Dugard could have been much shorter. After being kidnapped and kept prisoner for such an extended period, many believed that she had been added to the list of others who disappeared. However, many opportunities were missed in the search for the girl who was hidden in Garrido's house. This case is now an iconic example of missed opportunities for the benefit of law enforcement agencies and is a perfect illustration of the possible background that is a part of numerous cases of missing persons.

CHAPTER 7: YOSEMITE NATIONAL PARK

Yosemite National Park is one of the smallest parks that are open to public that covers just 1200 acres of total. It's a mix of cascades, valleys, Knolls, Sequoias wild, and very some time ago, glacial mass. The park is home to 3.7 million visitors travel to Yosemite every year to revel in the precipices of stone and natural diversity, and also an area for recreation with no any response. According to David Paulides, a main expert in Yosemite's National Park vanishings, Yosemite is perhaps the most significant group of people missing compared to others North American parks. About 45 people are believed to be missing the Yosemite National Park the region offers to the table. This is a many missing people with no information.

The seven most famous instances of Yosemite National Park will leave you with many questions. Did the person suffer some sort of mishap, injustice or some other issue? With no evidence of the cases mentioned above, one could speculate on the possible causes. Schema scholars will have you believe there's something wrong taking place in the parks of the public.

For example, why would someone who is a retired police officer and researcher be told he could not be able to access Stacy Arrass' file unless there was a reason to conceal something regarding her disappearance? Is it because the national park's attempt to safeguard Stacy's memory Stacy and her family's desire to keep the file sealed, or is there something else? There are many who believe that the public park framework is aware of more than they claim in a lot of cases that are not being investigated but wouldn't a better option be to conclude that without any evidence and the recreation facility isn't able to answer the question?

Dikran Knadjian

Dikran Knadjian, who was 20, was killed when he went on to die. disappearance. On the 24th of July 1972 Knadjian dressed in a blue, white, and red Polo shirt, paired with the blue bellbottom pants. Dikran was out in the nature in Curry Village, which is the most recent of his areas. People who witnessed the incident said they observed Dikran on the 24th of July but not the next day. Knadjian was a medical understudy taking a break during his time at Cambridge University. He also was planning to travel to Florida after he left the Yosemite area. The most important thing that had a serious awareness of his disappearance could he claim that he was being asked by the front work area or the camp's orderly for instructions on how to climb up towards Half Dome. Did he change his mind and start climbing somewhere else and that's the reason it was difficult to find him? Perhaps he had an issue with his body along the way towards Half Dome that left

He is difficult to locate?

Stacy Arrass

Stacy Arrass disappeared on July 25, 1981 in Yosemite National Park. She was spotted wearing T-shirt, stockings, an optics cap, cap and a camera. Stacy arrived on Yosemite with her dad , along with an entourage of six others. They were riding horses. Stacy told her dad that she would be taking pictures and inquired whether he wanted to join her. He wasn't interested but a man at the group, who was 72 years old of age, stated that she could go along. The man did not follow her throughout the entire journey. The slope was a bit steeper towards the lake, he slid down. The rest of the crowd appeared at the lake as Stacy was getting closer towards the lake. She walked by certain trees, then disappeared from view. After her father did not pay attention to her and her family, they were able to focus on her. They noticed her camera's lens a few inches away from the point where they did not concentrate on her. For a significant amount of time, searchers and police officers searched the area in search of clues to where she could be. The dogs were bred to track her path to the lake, but there was nothing.

Burt O'Ryan Dollar and Steven M. Clark

Dollar Clark and Clark are believed as missing in the south of Yosemite National Park. The two were preparing to set up campand were traveling in the White Ford Festiva with an Indiana tag. The two were reported missing on July 9 in 1995. Dollar was 20 years old. The recognizable features of his face include an appendectomy scar and a canine head tattoo and dark/tan shaded ink applied to the left shoulder of his front along with a dollar symbol on his left bicep. The most important information that can be recovered regarding Clark Dollar and Dollar is the car located off of the highway 395. The vehicle was situated on the Nevada-California highway, and was not far from the recreation zone. Clark aged 21 old age and had no marks or tattoos. It is generally accepted that they took an excursion to Yosemite due to it being their last location is Long Beach, California when they announced that they would go to an area for camping near Yosemite.

Do Dollar and Clark really go to Yosemite and did they opt to visit Nevada instead?

Kieran Burke

Kieran Burke went missing on the 5th of April, 2000. In the time of his disappearance, the man was aged 45 years old. His dark hair was becoming less on top, and he was dressed in an aircraft coat made of cowhide. Burke was at Yosemite National Park during a holiday, after having travelled from Dublin, Ireland. It has been discovered that he stayed at an inn close to the park's recreation area from April 4 until the 6th of April. The family is still seeking answers as Burke was an experienced and a ferocious climber. Burke was a couple with three children. The evidence of witnesses' articulations shows Burke was last found at Yosemite Valley at Curry Village. It was April 5 of 2000. When the police searched the vehicle, they only discovered the rental car that he had left in the Curry Village Lot. There was no evidence of Burke or his vehicle, and following an extensive search of the area where he was however, he's not present. The search within the recreation area did not begin until April 11. It was April 11. National Park requested anybody in the recreation area between the fifth and sixth of April to look through photos they took but no one has contacted to ask for information.

Michael Allen Ficery

Ficery had turned 51 years old on the 15th of June 2005, when he made his way into Yosemite National Park, gone for good. It was reported that the T-shirt he was wearing with sleeves that were ripped off and a torn scarf, which was his normal attire. Michael was able to climb on his own and was according to a recreation area officer, headed toward Hetch Hetchy reservoir. He was spotted following the trail that leads climbers through the north side of the reservoir. It was also realized that he changed his plan and then started up his Pacific Crest Trail. Park officers started an investigation on Tuesday following his disappearance since his family had been brought into. The wild grant he received expired on Sunday, which meant it was back to normal. The following day, the searchers rediscovered his backpack. It was grieving being deprived of geography guide, camera, and a Jug of water. The knapsack was discovered close to Tilltill Mountain, which incited the public park to employ canines, helicopters and helicopters as well as five region search and rescue groups. In addition to the rucksack there was no other trace of the item.

George Penca Jr.

George Penca is delegated missing/lost in the week of June 17th, 2011. Penca was last observed in dim running pants, white stripes and a dark T-shirt while perusing D&B at the back. Penca entered Yosemite National Park to climb to Yosemite Falls. It was discovered that he was at the top in Yosemite Falls. It was not like the any other Yosemite disappearances, Penca was with a Church group, and did not have any food or water in his possession. The public park searched for seven days and didn't track any evidence. The initial search began because of the fact that members of his community reported that he didn't return. On the weekend of the 18th day, the recreation center started a massive search of the fast area where he was last observed at. Around 105 people were searched.

and salvage workers was based in California and salvage workers from all over California to help. The hunt area was 70 square miles in the vicinity of Yosemite Falls. The area ranges from 4000 to 8000 feet above the ocean. On the 23rdof May, the recreation area agreed that the search efforts would be restricted by another method of search designed to be a part of Penca. Through the entire search nothing of any information or personnel items were found.

In this case there is a possibility that Penca fell close to the fall and his body was unable to control it and straying from the pursuit framework. Penca's family hopes that a resolution could be discovered in the near future.

The Conspiracy

A lot of websites believe that there's something going within Yosemite National Park, however no one is able to define exactly the nature of it. In the course of directing exploration, only 7 missing persons were identified, however Paulides states there are more than 40 missing instances, with no response. Some trick scholars would like to expose this "inconspicuous creature" that is the parks however it's a blight on families that are stressing over the disappearance of Yosemite. One reason that trick scholars continue going with their ideas is the reaction of scent and dead body dogs in the parks. A lot of meticulously trained canines will be on a course for a while before they move around and around or stop and then decline to carry in the same direction. Other plausible theories are possible for example, like getting off the search area that the park wasn't successful in finding an evidence of those missing. There is one thing that can never be not ruled out in these 7 cases, and that's animals being attacked because evidence like blood or tracks haven't been discovered in any of the locations where people were missing.

Rocky Mountain National Park

Rocky Mountain National Park offers numerous trails, campgrounds, and natural settings. In the areas from the lowlands to the tundras, people all all over the globe have taken part in the various peaks. Five guest areas as well as various ways to access the area of recreation, including three roads that are Highway 34, 36 and 7. The majority of visitors drive to the top of Trail Ridge Road to the highest point, which is 12,183 feet above sea level and look down on Estes Park. The entire park comprises comprised of 265, 761 pieces of land. Three or four million people go to the park each year in the springtime, and a large portion of the local population enjoy the recreation park throughout the year.

As per The Rocky Mountain Journal, from 1915 when the recreation area was constructed, until 2010 there were 344 park visitors died from accidents and self-destructing auto accidents, or disappearances. In 2014, an estimated 46 lives were assured in the recreation area due to the mountain ranges and the rivers. In the case of the deaths total, 60 deaths were recorded in Longs Peak, a treacherous mountain to climb even for a person with experience.

Estes Park as well as Big Thompson Canyon have overflowed in the ago. Through these catastrophes, people have lost their lives. The most recent flood, that was a major threat to the town in the beginning of the decade. It revealed not less than one body that was missing following the raging that was the Big Thompson in 1976. Joseph Laurence Halpern

Joseph Laurence Halpern is very likely to be dead, but only because it happened in the year 1933. Halpern was born on the 11th of September in 1910, and vanished on the 15th of August, 1933, making him age 22 at the time. In the present, if any evidence is discovered of his disappearance it will most likely contain his bones and perhaps some pieces of clothing. The man was said to wear a light blue shirt with light, earthy-colored pants. He wore heavy shoes along with a military backpack. Halpern had been climbing at Rocky Mountain National Park, close to Taylor Peak.

Halpern's case was analyzed similarly to the NPS practices of today. The NPS made an inquiry to the location in which he last appeared to have visited. They also advised any witnesses to forward information to local experts. The study yielded a number of leads that were not confirmed, including one that suggested Halpern was present located in Phoenix, Arizona in December 1934. Another report in 1935 mentioned Halpern working along with Lewis Brothers Circus around Michigan. A further document in the examination mentions that Halpern was a member of his Civil Conservation Corps in Nebraska. Halpern was known by several names of plumes, including Louis Hollenbuck, Teacher. Joseph left to the University of Chicago, worked at an observatory in Wisconsin and was said to be gifted in math, science and the study of cosmology. He was also an avid chess player.

Halpern was found missing by a fellow climber who set the camp along with Halpern. The person who was with him didn't climb the climb. When Halpern did not return after the hike, his friend informed specialists that he was missing. Unfortunately, when the report was made of a person who was missing, a snowstorm swept across the mountains, making it difficult to find any traces of Halpern in the search.

Due to the old age of the case, local experts are currently not investigating. The case remains open, and relatives have provided DNA samples in the event that his body is ever discovered.

Rocky Mountain National Park is an ideal place to explore different paths as well as waterways, mountains, and rivers. It was also the site of a major flood in the 1980s. Fall River flooded directly into downtown Estes Park. Given the various modifications the recreation park has supported in the years It is unlikely that the remaining parts of Halpern's body could ever be located. His family has not given up hope and trust that their DNA will one day or another prove valuable in the recognition of him.

Alfred Beilhartz

Beilhartz was just four years old when he disappeared on July 2nd 1938. The last time he was seen, he was near Fall River in Rocky Mountain National Park. His remains have not been found, not even when the area was flooded during the 80s. Alfred was one of eleven children. His family and he went fishing to Estes Park. They decided to hike along the rivulet. Alfred was a bit behind the rest members of the family. When they saw that he was suffering the loss of his family began looking over the road they were walking on. They called park officials to help. From the start park officers knew that the child was probably swept away into the rushing waterway. They declared the river a disaster and dragged it along for six miles in search of Alfred. During the search, they had to pull out the dam of a beaver to ensure Alfred was not trapped within the dam. The moment Alfred's body wasn't found in such a large search of the water, the officers thought it was necessary to search for smell dogs. The scent trail proved Alfred had gone missing just a little. However all signs stopped. The dogs walked a bit away, sat down, and stopped. The place was rocky and unpleasant.

Witnesses explained that two people saw what they believed to be the sound of a scream. They glanced around to check the child's face and were sure it was the child. Two thousand was more than the place Alfred went missing. They surveyed the edge that was higher than them. They discovered that they had seen Alfred who certainly looked similar to Alfred who was at Devils Nest. The recreation officers dealt with the witness's explanation with seriousness even though it seemed out of the ordinary to believe that Alfred being this high based on the place his family members were climbing. The officers employed climbing gear and surveyed the area in the vicinity of Devils Nest, just as diverse areas around Fall River, however never even thought of a body, or evidence of the location Alfred might have been.

Keith Reinhard and Tom Young

Keith Reinhard worked for the Daily Herald as a games essayist. He was in Silver Plume, Colorado from Chicago, Illinois in 1988. When he was in Silver Plume, Reinhard learned of his disappearance on the 7th of September, 1987. Tom Young was an inhabitant of the tiny mining town that was located near that of the Rocky Mountains. Last time Tom appeared was at the time he closed the book shop and took a walk in the mountain with his canine.

In no reason that is justifiable, Reinhard was extremely intrigued by Young 's story to the point where Reinhard resigned from having a job with The Daily Herald to open an antique shop in the same location to where Young's book store was. Reinhard began working on the plot of a novel in connection with Tom Young's disappearance, but the thing that makes the defense terrifying is that Reinhard disappeared too.

In the month of July in 1988 Tom Young 's remaining parts were discovered along with his canine. Youngful and his dog both suffered discharge wounds to the head. The gun was found on the scene, and neighbors believed Young killed his pet and then committed suicide.

Reinhard was aware of the hunted down assemblages of Young and his dog. He closed the and informed everyone that they would be moving to the top on Pendleton Mountain. Many thought his disappearance was odd , since he went up Pendleton Mountain at 4:30pm, which is a hike that takes an average of six hours. He did not dress appropriately or carry any equipment. Agents were looking over the mountain, and one of them tragically died after his plane was destroyed. Reinhard's obsession with is a problem. Many believe that he planned his disappearance to create his own unique vibe. It is also believed that they could have concluded the entire thing upon realizing that Young's situation was not as confusing as he thought it was. There are some rare kinds of people who think that the fact that he as well as Young were victims of injustice. It was thought

That Young was murdered and his death was planned as self-destruct to cover up the fact. People who believe in the theory that Reinhard noticed a clue and that the person responsible was able to help Reinhard in disappearing. This is unlikely because Reinhard himself has confirmed that he did climb Pendleton Mountain. The experts haven't found his body , nor have they found any evidence to suggest he's alive.

Yellowstone National Park

Yellowstone National Park is 3,400 square miles, and attracts more than two million people each year. Many of them travel from all over the globe to visit places such as Old Faithful as well as the animals like moose or buffalo. They also come to view the usual ponders that the recreation area has to offer guests, from glacial masses cut mountains to stunning streams. Yellowstone was a common area of residence for Native Americans. Since the land has been preserved and protected, the Native American legacy is additionally secured. Through four entry points into the recreation area, visitors are able to enter the park from Montana as well as Wyoming from the west, east south, north, and east. Every year, over of 20 visitors slough off the dust of Yellowstone National Park. The majority of these deaths are difficult to track due to the number of visitors who visit during the time of the event. There are more than 10 common ways to die in Yellowstone. Most people do not pay attention to the warnings for security and go too close to the springs and then succumb to the sulfur consuming by falling into. It is reasonable to assume that if someone disappears in this case, it was a creature or a fall off a high bluff, or mountain, on the trail of climbing or due to the incident that they fell into a pool of sulfur. This may be the reason for the men in this section or if Tom Young's case led to his disappearance. They could be able to have disappeared through different methods. According to Paulides the author, there are around nine cases connected to Yellowstone National Park that have no objective. However, there were a few found through the internet.

The Unknown Man

Every now and then, when someone close to you or a family member disappears from a recreation space there is no basis that they disappear however, since they're not identified by experts. The passageway in Yellowstone offers a variety of ways people have been able to kick the bucket in the park, from freak accidents, like lightning strikes, to sinking into underground Aquifers. In 1920, park officials discovered the body of one man. The mysterious man sat to the death in Hellroaring Creek around 1.5 miles within the northern boundary of Yellowstone. It's unclear that he threw the bucket in addition to what his name was. The body was found on 21st April 1920. The temperature was severe for quite a long time, and the police were unable to decide when the man sunk the bucket, as the ice and the rogue virus can usually keep the body. All the officers had to do was to bury the body in a grave close to the location where he was found. They marked the grave with stakes placed at the foot and head, and created an impression on the nearby tree.

The man's subtleties were recorded which included the fact that he was 5'5" 120 pounds and was about 40 years old. age. His dark hair was long and mustache. The fact that he was not set in stone is that he threw the bucket due to frozen feet, leaving him handicapped to the point that it was impossible to get out of the recreation area. The most important reason for why the reason he didn't disappear forever was a complaint by another person in Yellowstone which revealed the presence of bleeding tracks. The report did not specify what tracks guests at the recreation areas was able to see.

Park officers released the story to mediaoutlets, however, no one ever approached them to confirm that they had met the man. The park officers assumed he was an outsider who was visiting this area of the USA as well as Yellowstone.

Dennis Eugene Johnson

Dennis Johnson was eight years old when he went missing within Yellowstone National Park. The date was on July 12 in 1966. His family was in the park that is open to the public in Inyoken, California. The family members watched him go during the Cascade Picnic Area near Canyon Village. The family tried to search for him after he failed to return to the area for cooking or show up when they were calling him. The case files show that there was a lack of evidence to find him. There was not much knowledge of the investigation and the possibility of salvaging at that time However the NPS has established conventions which generally concern individuals as well as hunt networks and even dogs.

Bruce Pike

The 47-year-old entered Yellowstone National Park around the Indian Creek camping area on August 2nd on the 2nd of August, 2006. At first, located in Texas, Bruce Pike vanished disappeared forever, along with many others who set into a park that is not a public one. The only evidence found by Pike was his car, that was in Yellowstone and was driving experts to discover he vanished from a location near.

Stuart Isaac

Stuart Isaac's black Lexus was discovered on the 26th of September however the fact that he was last observed on September 12 2010, within Yellowstone National Park. The vehicle was found in Craig Pass, which is one of the lower Yellowstone National Park terrific circle streets. He was 48 years old age, with hair that was short-edited, three tattoos, and possibly the appearance of a mustache. After observing the vehicle abandoned, officers ordered a search through the area to find the possibility that he walked away off the car. The NPS have not found any evidence of the location Isaac might be. The last time his family saw him was after the time he quit Burtonsville, Maryland for a cross-country journey.

CHAPTER 8: GREAT SMOKY MOUNTAINS DISAPPEARANCE

Great Smoky Mountains National Park is vital to The Blue Ridge Mountains and the more extensive Appalachian Mountain Chain. It is formed around North Carolina and Tennessee. It comprises 522,419 acres of land which is the largest guaranteed public parks within the in the region. Between 9 and 11 million visitors and residents go to the area for recreation every year, which is twice more than that the Grand Canyon gets. The sheer number of people who visit could mean that many people are swept away or vanish from the park. The six cases discussed in this article are among the most confusing cases because there is no evidence that has been located. The victims basically disappeared in the majority of cases in the eyes of other. The absence of evidence of creature attacks or any other explanation was considered as a major factor in the majority of these instances. The mountain pinnacles could be less imposing than the ones from these

Rocky Mountains or Alaskan parks that are discussed within this publication, however it doesn't mean that the territory is less tolerant.

Dennis Martin

Dennis was along with three other boys when he vanished on the 14th of June in 1969. He was just six years old age, and the three young men were staying at Great Smoky Mountains National Park along with members of the Martin family. The boys admitted to being isolated from the rest of the family in some tricks; regardless, Dennis didn't return. A massive pursuit was arranged but no trace was observed. One person who was watching said that he saw a man with a rough appearance walking through the woods in the late evening, shortly after shouting. The report was not confirmed.

A few years later, the man was hunting in the woods. He said he was observing bones that grew the form of a child, but he did not report the sight immediately. If all else is equal He waited until the 1980s to ensure that he wouldn't be punished for hunting. If a hunt was conducted to the"assumed" area with bones, nothing could be located. It's unclear on the possibility that the other pieces were from Dennis Martin, of another entity, or even a tale the man fabricated.

Trenny Lynn Gibson

Seven years after Martin disappeared, Trenny Lynn Gibson disappeared. The last sighting she had was on the 18th of October in 1976. Trenny was 16 years old, and was at the recreation facility with the school's understudies. The group was climbing as part of an Bearden High School class journey. Students were heading toward Clingmans Dome up to Andrews Bald. Gibson was turning around to the parking areaand was walking by himself. The school had divided the climbers and there was rumours that there were masses of people actually ascending the path the Trenny was taking down. But, no one in front of her or behind her claimed they had seen her. The pursuit was swift and began with scent dogs, and took Gibson's route to the highway before ending. After a long investigation, the recreation center ended the hunt. The scent trail recommends Gibson visited the parking area , and later took off in a car regardless of whether through the decision or through foul play.

Thelma Pauline Melton

September 25, 1981 was to have been the final time anyone was able to see Thelma Melton. Thelma was assigned the status of missing or lost. This is not like the majority of public park posts that are generally characterized as considered to be imperiled missing. The usual posting says missing or imperiled. Melton was found to be suffering from hypertension and subsequent sickness. Melton was on prescription for both of these issues that park professionals believed could be the reason she wasn't able to quit the park alive.

Melton had been climbing in the company of two other people. They were last seen at four p.m.. Thelma expanded her speed, walking ahead of her companions. They watched her cross a hill on the way. The group of friends accepted her return to the camping area at which they were able to see that their Airstream campsite was set back. Around 4:45 p.m. her companions were back in the camp area but Thelma wasn't there to be observed. Her partner was in the trailer, waiting for the trio to return.

The group surveyed the area quickly but when they were unable to see her, they reported her disappearance at 6 after 6 pm.. She was aware of the area, particularly Deep Creek Trail. Park experts didn't notice signs that she had strayed from the trail. There was nothing unusual with regard to her routines. The most significant deviation from her usual routine was that she was not able to contribute at the senior establishment that she typically served dinners. On September 24, she ruled against the idea. The judge also refused to allow her to drive a vehicle due of her condition. Her spouse had the keys for the trailer. Melton went strolling identification.

The couple she was with were have been destructive, despite being aware that their medical background had a few minor problems with melancholia. A couple of years prior to her disappearance she was on Valium. As of today, she was not taking the drug at the time she vanished and, however the fact that her partner's Valium solution was not present when her significant other disappeared. It's not clear whether she had taken the drug.

The pills are on the rise. The woman was also expressing her frustration about the lack of mother, according to her mother's advice.

The older place stated that she had made a phone decision on the day prior to her disappearance, which was quite surprising because she had never used the phone. The pastor also thought that she was in a non-sanctioned affair, but no evidence was found to support the theory. The other information was not discovered and the case is unsolved.

Michael Edwin Hearon

Michael Edwin Hearon vanished August 23rd, 2008 as he was walking near close to the Great Smoky Mountains National Park. The reports indicate Hearon went home around 11 a.m. and was heading towards Bell Branch on a 4-wheeler toward Abrams Creek Campground. The neighbors were able to see the man. It was normal because his 100-acre residence was attached to the recreation zone. Mike who got pleasure from the opportunity to be named, also informed his two kids know that he was leaving at the Maryville, Tennessee townhouse to visit his home at Happy Valley. He planned to cut and bramble his hoard. He was there with virtually no money, medication or

The idea that she was a selftrimmer. at Andy's child then he took it and put the cutter in his truck. The neighbors also saw Mike arrive with his trailer and truck carrying the cutter. It was just 15 minutes following his arrival when he was spotted by his neighbors getting out the four-wheeler.

A few bizarre incidents have family members wondering about the day Hearon was last seen. In the normal course, he would remove the trailer's cutter and place the trailer and truck closer to home. However, when guests came to look at dairy cattle on a Sunday they saw that the truck was still filled with.

Mike's parents also resided on the property that was adjacent to it, therefore they visited Mike on Sunday, only to get no response. Then they went back on Monday. At this point, they were extremely anxious as the truck was still in the spot it was on Sunday, and nobody was looking at the entrance. His parents noticed that the house was not secured. They looked around both inside and outside. Inquired, but focusing on the most likely scenario Mike's family members called Mike's child Matt. Matt took a look at the room to see the cruiser and vehicle at the moment in the carport , and nothing looked out of place.

When they inspected the house further they found keyholes, money cut using credit cards, permits and cash, as well as his cell phone and gun inside the truck. Matt as well Andy were definitely concerned so they went to the farm. Matt along with Andy were certainly worried and walked to the farm. The farm has wheelers The two men decided to take a look at the more than 75 parcels of land However,

Couldn't find anything.

At this point, it was obvious that Mike did not return and did not seem to be in a state of readiness to go back. Police were called. After a lengthy search, the vehicle on which Mike was riding was located one mile from his residence. The date was set for August 26. The ATV was unharmed in any way, but it was found in a high incline with the start switch still on.

Hearon did not claim the land the ATV was considered to be located on. It wasn't even in the same street that he typically took. There was no evidence to suggest that a mishap or attack on a creature had occurred. There was no evidence of unfairness. In fact, there wasn't any sign whatsoever.

Hundreds of volunteers and emergency laborers would scour the area for seven days, using ATVs, ground-based lookouts and helicopters, as well as horsebacks as well as body dogs. Mike Hearon's passport and all evidence that was relevant to his case were found in his home. There was no issue or secret information have been discovered to explain reasons Hearon could have left his home. His family is seeking the reasons behind the sudden disappearance of Hearon. They are pondering what happened after being at home He decided to pull out his four-wheeler rather than taking the mower out for emptying.

Christopher Lee Cessna

Christopher Lee Cessna was identified as missing from Great Smoky Mountains close to Wake, North Carolina. He was reported missing at the age of 45. old and had no distinctive features. There is not much information available in the case beyond a single number. It's apparent that his family members reported the missing person on April 27 in 2011. This wasn't the only missing person's situation that the park's public officials were working on at the time however it occurred prior to the incident that involved David Harrington. David Harrington was found and his case closed. The park's public administration informed Knox News know when they saw the body of Harrington that they would reduce the Cessna examination because there was nothing found in the lengthy search for Cessna. For a very long period of time, police and search dogs swept the area where Cessna's 2009 Audi was discovered by officers who examined his identification. All they could find was the car in the Newfound Gap leaving region. There is no evidence as to whether Cessna was climbing and suffered a fatal accident or simply became one of the disappeared. Since 2015, no new information has been provided in the case. Derek Joseph Lueking

On March 17, 2012, Derek Lueking disappeared. His last location is Cherokee,

North Carolina. It has also been suggested that he went missing within Smoky Mountain National Park, which is located on the Tennessee and North Carolina state line. Derek left the Microtel Inn along with Suites parking lot on the 17th of March. The vehicle was discovered in the park that was open to the public. The problem with his disappearance is the possibilities of a myriad of questions. There was no one was in the Newfound Gap region parking garage was able to verify if they saw him walking along through the area's recreation trails. The car was reported leaving from the Microtel around 4.30 a.m.. There is a huge distance between the hotel and the park that is public. The administration of the recreation area is currently trying to find answers but there's close to nothing and there was no massive pursuit initiated. The vehicle may be taken towards the recreation area by a different person and that would suggest that, between and the Microtel along with the automobile that was discovered, Derek met with injustice. The only thing that police and NPS have to do are speculations.

CHAPTER 9: ALASKA NATIONAL PARK DISAPPEARANCES

Alaska is a harsh place to live, whether inside one of massive urban areas or in the wilderness. It's definitely not the place for those who prefer to stay away from the world outside. When going on an adventure, it's best to not leave a plan or join a group because one doesn't know what may happen. Mining in particular regions of Alaska has created risky openings, tunnels for mining and much more. Mountain bears, moose, brown bears, and grizzly bears be a danger to those who climb or walk. For those who are missing of the Alaska National Parks they have realized how difficult a location in Alaska can be regardless of the season is winter or summer. In the cities, it is forbidden to wander along paths that are forested that are laden with food as bears are often seen in the city areas in search of an easy food source. Denali National Park

Denali National Park is one of the biggest North American national parks at 6 million acres. The majority of the park is wilderness terrain, with just one street that is separated from the park. This within Alaskan park has the 400,000 people who visit annually to hike, observe wildlife and canine sledding. It also offers cross-country skiing, and snow-friendly travel. For those who live in the mountains the most prominent peak can be found on Mount McKinley standing 20,320 feet above sea level, making it the highest point on the continent of North America. Based on the measurements taken between 1903 and 2012, 120 people perished in Denali attempt to scale Mount McKinley. Since 2012, 44 bodies have not been found, and a many are believed to be missing, believed dead. The majority of victims of Denali National Park are with at least a small groups that can provide clear record of what happened. Two cases have been discovered during the research process that do not provide strong opinions about Denali and the surrounding regions of Denali. Hiroko Nemoto

Hiroko Nemoto was a student in Michigan State University in 1998. She lived within East Lansing and going to classes, however, she was an Japanese public. Nemoto decided to take an excursion in Anchorage, Alaska, taking an excursion on June 3rd 1998. Nemoto was on a Northwest Airlines flight came to Alaska. Specialists were then able to confirm that Nemoto was in Denali National Park and Preserve close to Mount McKinley. The next step on her schedule was

An unintentional stay at a small hotel situated in Anchorage prior to her departure for Wasilla.

Wasilla is located 50 miles to the to the north from Anchorage. Police investigating her disappearance discovered she was in the Windbreak Hotel in Wasilla on June 8th in 1998. The hotel also had a restaurant where she was eating with a male on June 9th. According to the investigation, the man drove her from the bus station, where she was hoping to catch the bus towards Denali Park. Nemoto disappeared for ever. The experts couldn't determine whether she had walked into the recreation park because no one at the time could claim they'd observed her.

In the course of the investigation the evidence was discovered that she had purchased an Alaskan train ticket between Anchorage up to Whittier, Alaska. In addition, she purchased an air ticket between Whittier up to Valdez, Alaska.

There are many factors that make it appear like Nemoto tried to disappear intentionally. In the beginning she was always talking to her mom every week. Nemoto told a fellow student at the university that she did not plan on returning to Japan However, she never informed her parents or her friends returning home of her plans. The person who was with her informed agents that Nemoto declared she'd be returning to Michigan after a month being in Alaska. But, Hiroko just bought a single direction ticket to Anchorage.

One of the companions, which is not clear if it is an identical companion. Let police be aware that Nemoto said she was not planning of returning at Michigan State University for the next semester, despite reality that she had been and contemplating getting her major in brain research. Nemoto obviously stated that she believed that the flow and ebb method would allow her to conduct research, and she was required to become an analyst in clinical practice all other things being equally. Another companion also said Nemoto was the one who took most of her clothes and other personal assets when she went away. The companion along with her partner had dinner together the evening she left for Alaska. It was evident that the trip was designed to be a re-visit of Japan. One of the interviewees stated that Nemoto was awarded a lower grade than she anticipated in her spring semester, and believed that it could have prevented Hiroko in her studies despite having a deficit of 10 credits to the degree she earned at undergrad.

Alaska isn't referred to as"the "Last Frontier" for nothing. It's an unexplored region in North America. When a person moves away from larger urban areas to join some of the more small networks, it's possible to disappear. The manner in which Michigan State University companions realized that she was not ready to go back to school , and similar to one realized that she was heading for Alaska in a few months suggests that Nemoto could be a victim of a snitch.

Have decided to not go back home to Michigan as well as Japan. As a meeting substudy is required, she must obtain the Visa to stay in America or travel to a place where there is no need to investigate reports. It's unclear if police have a suspicion of the rat. They may be able to chip away at the proof of ticket and also the questions they asked in various locations she could have visited.

Gerald Myers

Sometimes family and friends will have an different perceptions with regard to the proper goal after the person disappears. Gerald Myers is most certainly one of those instances. It's not so much the family and friends of Gerald Myers do not want to hear each and every detail to his disappearance, but for his traditional law partner she believes he's somewhere on the mountain that which he went but was missing from. She believes that he's gone and believes he's on the grave of his "legitimate" grave because the mountaineering was his passion.

Myers was at Denali National Park right outside of Anchorage on the 19th of May 2009. He was with a group of fellow mountaineering friends who needed to conquer the gruelling Mount McKinley. Myers left the camp, but not with his fellow comrades. After all the note he left behind which read, "I'm happening the extent that I'm able to safely go." He carried his skis at the 19,200-foot camp. A number of climbers who were sliding on the mountain, that day wrote about the time they witnessed Gerald move towards the highest elevation of 20,320 feet. point.

When no of his climbing companions were able to contact them, they reported the missing man. The searchers were found, but did not find any evidence of a raging glissade or snow cavern Myers may have built. For six days , heroes tried to discover any clue of where he might have fallen or disappeared from the mountain. In 33 hours flying time and 3,000 top-of-the-line aeronautical images, no trace or trace of Gerald Myers was ever found.

In the case of Mount McKinley this isn't an unusual situation. There have been many attempts to climb up to its highest point only to cause a disaster to occur and in a way. Most of the time, there's an idea of what happens to climbers who attempt to climb Mount McKinley. When bodies are discovered, they are however they are not for Gerald Myers that isn't true. His family members are left to inquire about why he would make the decision to climb on his own based on his previous experience. He was sure not to take alone, but was it because he was too high and low in oxygen which caused him to act out in a way that was unreasonably? Could it be that he wanted to create the mountain as his final resting place? The only thing his family members are left with thoughts of outrage, grief, and sorrow.

Glacier National Park and Patrick Whalen

Patrick Whalen disappeared in Glacier National Park. It's only a couple of hours away from

Anchorage towards the south. The park that is open to the public is a landmark for Alaska and, in particular, for those who were raised watching the television series Glacier Bay. Icy mass Park has a list of 260 people who have passed away from a variety of reasons. The record began in January 1913. A news report reveals the time frame of loss of lives at around 260. It is not the general passings or disappearings are as perplexing like whalen Patrick's. Joe Prince in 1913 is famous for having sat to death when snowshoeing. Four other people have jumped the bucket due to their vulnerability to a baffling virus. A Glacial

Mass National Park records the main five causes of death, which include the point of suffocation, climbing, coronary failure, vehicle accident or a fall on climbing. Self-destruct has been the claim of six people, as proven by the report's insightful findings.

Of the 260 individuals in the count for 2013 13 are considered as dead and absent. It is discovered that two of the 13 were at Lake McDonald in 1923. Two explorers in 1924 were found as lost in the middle of Granite Park and Lake McDonald. Another man disappeared in 1933, after he had climbed Mount Brown. One of the people on the rundown was thought to have disappeared of Goat Haunt by 1934. Two anglers were fishing on Lake Kintla in 1950 never to be ever seen again.

The Rising Sun Motor Inn representative was believed to have fallen out of St. Mary Falls in 1964. In the year 1976, a couple with five kids was located in the Apgar excursion region near Lake McDonald, never to hear from for the rest of their lives. Their boat was found on the western shores of the

Lake in a secluded area between rocks, with their propeller stuck within the sedimentary rock.

The passing occurred later in 2003. The Robert Fire might have asserted Larry Kimble. His truck was located near Rocky Point Trailhead near Fish Creek Campground in June 2003 and the fire started in July. Park officials have concluded that the body of the deceased may be located in an area that was later smoldering due to the fire. the remains.

As of 2001 Patrick Whalen was recorded as missing, presumed to be dead, and presumed dead by Glacier National Park officers. At the time , he was 33 years old. The truck was discovered near Kiowa Junction on US 89 in November 2001. Prior to May, park officials spotted an illegal camp near Atlantic Creek that had Whalen's assets. Police believed that Whalen had vanished from the camp, but when they saw his vehicle , they weren't sure what to conclude. Did he drive his truck to go to a different area away from the camp but didn't return? Did someone see his truck empty in a close-by location and steal it? The answer is rooted in Whalen's disappearance. Kevin O'keefe

Kevin O'Keefe, from Sacramento, California, is additionally a person protected through Glacier Bay National Park. The disappearance of his body occurred in 1985. The case summary has been distributed to the general public. The NPS report says that officers inspected O'Keefe's tent. It was damaged by a focus shaft, however the tent itself was missing. After the tent's announcement officers went back to determine if something was causing the trouble. They believed that O'Keefe could be back. They also conducted an air - and land search in an try to locate other clues regarding his disappearance. The family members of his disappeared friend said they would typically go on short climbs during the day from his campsite. Because his camping cot and backpack were in the campsite, officers believed they could have guessed that he planned to go to a climb for the day instead of a quick exploration.

A problem with the test occurred when they saw his sew cap and boots about a hundred yards of the camp. A well-trained camper would never take off his footwear in Alaska in the first place, not even in the event that the person was in a rational state of mind. There is no evidence to support an attack by a creature because his food was pristine from creatures as officers scoured through the area and then a short time later after they arrived back at the camp site to set up.

Glacier National Park records 10 of the 260 crossings that bears have killed as a result of a collision. The reason why thirteen of them are not included in that rundown or dare for being killed by a beast is the order in which they went or the way they went missing. Evidently, a few deaths are attributed to the Lake however, the individuals who were climbing and climbing or setting up camp fell or experienced something else. The killing of a creature would leave marks, like tracks, damaged assets and blood, that scent canines can track.

CHAPTER 10: HAWAII NATIONAL PARK

Hawaii Volcanoes National Park actually is home to a spring that is bubbling lava, despite of the fact it hasn't seen an eruption in the past. The highest pinnacle can be found at Mauna Loa with a culmination of 56,000 feet above the bottom of the ocean, which is a sluggish. This means that Mauna Loa 27,000 feet taller than Mount Everest. It is also the highest mountain in the world in terms of volume, at less than 20000 cubic miles. The recreation zone was established in 1916. It encompasses 323,431 acres of land, with less than 1.5 million people visiting every year. The same is true for other parks that are public the mortality rates are quite high but there are also clues like the situation in 2015 in which a 11-year-old child disappeared from Hawaii National Park yet was finally discovered alive.

John Cameron Reece

The 25th of November, 1999 was an excellent time in the life of John Cameron Reece given his disappearance out of Volcanoes National Park. Reece worked as an expert in the United States Geological Survey Biological Resources Division. He was part in the Hawaii Mauna Loa region group. His residence was close to Hawaii Volcanoes National Park, located situated outside Hilo. He was working away at Palila's Palila reclamation project when he went missing. his disappearance.

Reece was planning to do an extended climb from Thanksgiving until Sunday. He informed his friends that he planned to ascend from the North Kohala's Pololu Valley to Waipio Valley in Hamakua. He asked that an assistant provide him with a ride from Keaau on the 25th which is where he'd begin the climb. The understudy informed specialists that he took Reece in the morning at around 7 a.m.. He also informed police that Reece was dressed in a light shaded t-shirt as well as jeans and cover boots. He was also seen carrying the red Kelty Redwing bag with equipment for downpours, canvas camping oven, lounger as well as four days worth of meals.

Reece revealed his plan to the people closest to him who were close to him, and he decided to hike Awini Trail. He would hike only a few miles away of Waimanu Valley, blindsiding his direction. After a while, Reece began his journey, heavy rainstorms began. Agents thought it was a risky path as the course has a number of dangers, including high inclines.

One witness approached to say the man who was wearing Reece's illustration a ride approximately twelve p.m.. The man stated that the person was dropped off at Kawaihae near the intersection of the road Waimea-Kawaihae and Queen Kaahumanu State Highway. Reece didn't respond to be able to help at the time of the 29th of November. The USGS

He was reported that he was missing. The experts surveyed the region where he was last seen in. They inspected Hokokane Iki Valley as well as the USGS lodge that is located nearby. The lodge was built to aid abandoned explorers which meant that food and other provisions were in the vicinity. It is possible to think about that if Reece was able to climb up to the top of the hill to escape the rain There would be evidence. The hunt team didn't discover any unusual influences in the lodge to suggest Reece stopped at the lodge. Everyone agreed that 22-year-old Reece was reliable and skilled climber. Reece was born in Duncanville, Texas. He was working for USGS as an intern. USGS in the capacity of an intern. Timothy Joseph Lynch

Timothy Lynch was visiting Volcanoes National Park in Hawaii when he disappeared on June 6th on the 6th of June, 2003. He was a native from Newburgh, Indiana, Lynch was in Hawaii. Lynch was noticed by people at around 9:45 a.m. as well as 9:45 a.m. near the end the Chain of Craters Road. Experts noticed that his car abandoned in the spot. The spouse who was a divorcee announced that he was missing. Just a year later the date was December 4, 2004, when she declared him legally dead. His spouse was really looking at his email reply because she actually knew the code. It appears that she was checking for messages on behalf of her, but the report doesn't mention. She checked her messages several hours after Lynch was believed to have been absent and was notified via Royal Kona Resort. This message led her to report Lynch missing. He didn't return however he also did not settle on the retreat. It was reported that the Royal Kona Resort was endeavoring to reach Timothy Lynch to decide when they would take a look and settle the bill. Furthermore, his return ticket for June 6 was never used. Police did not find anything during the search around Hawaii National Park, the rental car, or the resort. Hiromichi Yoshino

Hiromichi Yoshino, 51, was missing when his disappearance occurred in February of 2013. He was a Japanese visitor to this island was recently seen admiring Volcanoes National Park. Leave specialists located his vehicle rental outside the area of recreation, but despite the area the vehicle was located in was a sour and extremely sharp. A region that is considered to be dangerous police advised other visitors and residents not to look into the area. In February of 2013, five people were suffocated to death, several other people jumped the gun in car accidents and two fell off the cliffs.

After the vehicle was discovered and opened, it was found with a piece on the passenger side. It was written by Hiromichi Yoshino's writing on the back. They also uncovered money and a receipt for entry into the recreation center on February 13 , at 8.57 a.m.. The keys

They were discovered at the beginning in the rear of the car.

Police asked witnesses for any information they could have to share regarding the man's disappearance. Police were able to pursue Yoshino to a boardinghouse for the night at Volcano Village, however that was the only issue they could determine about his trip to Hawaii.

CONCLUSION

The sheer number of reported cases of missing persons is enough to leave one in awe. The idea that someone you know, a relative, or a beloved one, or even may disappear is a possibility seldom thought about, but the statistics show that it is higher than plane crashes and shark attacks. Due to this, those cases that truly capture the public's attention are ones that are involving the unanswered or the bizarre and the thrilling or the terrifying. With the number of people who go missing each year, there is never an abundance of cases.

We have learned throughout this book the potential for being an individual who is missing isn't restricted to criminals only and people that put their lives in danger's way. For each Dan Cooper stealing money with a hijacked aircraft and an Jaycee Dugard that was arrested then tortured and released through luck and luck. As it is beneficial to people to disappear and disappear from society but for others, it's an affliction that comes on them while they could be taking a walk to their school, or laying in bed.

This is perhaps the reason why events like these grab the attention of the public quickly. Not only do we have the ability to feel for the disappearing as well, but our hearts also extend to those left with no trace and who have to search over years in spite of the absence of evidence. Although the news cycle shifts and the media is able to shift to a new story there are people who are unable to admit the reality of what is. Even in the most difficult of situations like the one of Jaycee There is the possibility that our beloved relatives could return. Even at the worst instances, the stories of missing demonstrate a crucial human trait and are stories that are able to reach even the hardest of hearts.

The issue of missing people can be easily resolved. Similar to what has happened for many centuries the people are still able to disappear from the world. Even with modern technology, we're faced with the fact that at times there is nothing to do to trace our loved relatives. No matter if we blame criminals the people who are missing themselves accidents, or the supernatural cases of the missing frequently reveal more about us than we ever thought.

CPSIA information can be obtained
at www.ICGtesting.com
Printed in the USA
BVHW050851080223
658122BV00007B/104